"Has wisdom awakened you today?"

Praise for "World Tour of Wisdom"

"So long as you cling to it you can't go wrong!
The Truth has come."
— Islam

"The wise man ever delights in it,
the disciple in training will investigate it."
— Buddhism

"The Master has spoken."
— Confucianism

"This is the Way, the Truth, and the Life."
— Christianity

"It reveals the supreme secret of spiritual union."
— Hinduism

"Finally! 'A Guide That *Won't* Perplex!'"
— Judaism

Published by Chicago Press

Do not ignore something
that is said
just because of who says it.

Confucius

A WORLD TOUR of WISDOM

Finding Inner Peace

DAVID JAMES

Also by David James

A
DIVINE & SUBLIME
INTERVIEW
ABOUT
TIME

SHADOWS *and* LIGHT

SERVICE
for the age of
CELESTIAL SPEEDUP

LOVE IS BY
GOD
A WORLD TOUR *of* WISDOM
for FINDING INNER PEACE

A WORLD TOUR *of* WISDOM

Finding Inner Peace

Chicago Press

DAVID JAMES

Chicago Press
Phoenix, Arizona
chicagopress@greenleafbookgroup.com

ISBN: 1-929774-02-8   Paperback

First Chicago Press printing November 2000

Library of Congress Catalog Card number: 00-107875

Greenleaf Book Group LLC
660 Elmwood Point
Auroar, Ohio 44202

Printed in the United States of America

For you, reader,
so that you may
live life free of
all illusions,
find your own voice of holiness,
and live with everlasting joy.
Peace.

Contents

Preface

*A book without a preface is
like a body without a soul.*

— Hebrew Proverb

People

seldom

ever

change.

Krishnamurti

Before We Begin

A new age is beginning in human history. Each one of us has an exciting part to play on the world stage as this new era begins. That's because each one of us is going to be held accountable for our actions whether we like it or not. It doesn't matter who you are, what you look like, what you believe, what you want, why you think you're here, or what you do for a living, how much money you have, how much you pray, how many stock options you have, what your car is, who you have sex with, what your mistakes and sins are, or any of that external stuff – we will experience the consequences of our actions. The external world is undergoing massive changes because we are experiencing massive changes within ourselves. This change is a fact. It has nothing to do with opinions of either a secular or religious nature. Facts are facts, even though I know a lot of people hate hearing them. Tough.

As a Gen-Xer I have had enough of the doom and gloom that some people have put into the world, and that is why I wrote this book. I want to prove to people once and for all that there is plenty of proof to show that there are more similarities between any two people, spiritual masters, business gurus, religions, and nations than there are differences. Timeless wisdom can be found everywhere and in everyone. We only need to be interested long enough to apprehend it for ourselves, make it our own, and apply it to our life. Maybe then the world could be a bit brighter, lighter, and more fun for all of us. Interested?

This is not about anger, venting, or getting revenge on the previous generations. It is about communicating, sharing, expressing feelings, and most of all it is about accepting the wisdom that has been given to *all of us*. This is about sharing, love, the Golden Rule, and future hopes. I think I have collected more than enough evidence to convince you that love – the highest wisdom – is for everyone, everywhere, no exceptions! But if you don't want to listen to me, then go on and ignore what is said just because of who says it. Don't listen to Confucius' advice on that one.

People are waking up on a mass scale, becoming more accountable and responsible for their thoughts, feelings, perceptions, and actions. A new frequency is in the air and it is not a weak, garbled, fuzzy transmission. It has clarity, strength, a mission, critical mass, chutzpah, charisma, values, and it is currently bursting forth into mass consciousness – much to the chagrin of some other hacks from the old school of doom and gloom about the coming threat of *annuit coeptis novus ordo seclorum* (found on the back of the one dollar bill). Why would a New World Order, a global marketplace, a One-World community be so bad if it was to be based on wisdom? Well, move over preachers of doom, your time has come!

We are being introduced to a truly global marketplace and also to a global village in which a new conversation will be born. Throughout the last millennium there have been renaissances, enlightenments, dark ages, a cold war, two world wars, and too many other battles. Previous chapters in human history were about waging war while ignoring the fragility, diversity, and wonder of life. But a new age is unfolding in the human storyline. It is the dawn of disillusionment with the status quo, ushering in a new era of world peace.

The next phase of human consciousness is about realizing that peace is no longer one of many options. It is *the* option. Intellectually, we know the principles of peace. It is time to put those principles into application. It is time to walk the talk. It is time to be brutally honest with ourselves.

We must realize that any little compromises with peace and truth we make along the way are not-so-subtle cues to our children that we can talk a good talk (and Hollywood will definitely sell it), but sooner or later we have to actualize peace. Otherwise peace is merely an idea. Otherwise we can allow our children to become increasingly disillusioned with adults. Adults run the world, yet children are forced to suffer the mistakes of adults. How mature and responsible is this?

Let's take a look at some facts about the status quo,

the way things have been going. It doesn't matter whether you like it or not, it doesn't matter whether you believe it or not, but facts speak for themselves. Your feelings and beliefs *about* reality are irrelevant because reality just is. Get it? It's a "fact thing."

Unfortunately, because we decided not to look at reality in the first place and blind ourselves with reckless ambition and stupid ideologies from the dead-and-gone era of ancient times, we ended up avoiding reality at all costs. It seems that people have been too preoccupied with themselves at the expense of others. Even the name of the "self-help movement" has a tinge of selfishness about it. I think it's time for the "help-the-person-in-front-of-you movement" to pick up where the latter left off (if it's even over yet). If we don't do this, we will have to deal with the effects of our actions (or lack thereof). And let's get real about the consequences, folks: they are closing in on us at an alarming rate. We need less reaction and more action. We need more wisdom, less opinions. We need more intelligence about what everyone wants and needs and less arrogance and ignorance about excluding some people from love. That is not wise.

Once again, whether we like it or not, whether we believe it or not, your beliefs about the status quo are irrelevant and your opinion about it is meaningless. Beliefs and opinions without thinking and reasoning are what got us into this whole mess in the first place. What we need more than new beliefs about what we *have done* are new actions about what we *will do*. After we take a look at what "is," we will take a look at the wisdom of the ages for ways of solving any problems still lurking about. So what is this mess that is causing so much trouble today? What does it look like? Who does it affect? Let's see...

According to the FBI, between 1990 and 1997 the total crime rate fell 15.4 percent. But between 1960 and 1997, the total crime rate rose more than 160 percent. How does this affect the children? The FBI also notes that between 1990 and 1996 the juvenile violent crime arrest rate increased by 11 percent. Between 1965 and 1996 the rate increased 215 percent. Although the teenage abortion rate has decreased 28 percent between 1990 and 1996, it increased 27 percent between 1973 and 1996. Between 1990 and 1998 the percentage of high school seniors using illegal drugs increased 13 percent. But, overall illegal drug use has decreased only slightly between 1975 and 1998. And these are just the reports for the United States of America. How does the USA fair on the world stage?

According to Francis Fukuyama in *The Great Disruption*, the USA ranked as the nation with the fifth highest violent crime rate in the world. New Zealand had the highest followed by Canada, Sweden, England, and then the USA. In 1996 the violent crime rate was 63.4 violent crimes per 10,000 people. What's the problem and how do we solve it? Can we solve it together? What is the solution?

Let's take a trip and visit the past for a little bit, shall we?

"The Earth is but one country and mankind its citizens." This is a quote from Baha'u'llah, of the Baha'i religion, who lived in Iran in the nineteenth century. This faith affirms that God spoke to certain divine messengers around the world, spreading wisdom in many different forms and languages. The Baha'i tradition is based on economic justice, equal rights for everyone, education for everyone in order to eliminate ignorance, and the eradication of all barriers of race, class, and creed. How do these goals sound to you? Do they sound reasonable or just evil and cult-like? Think about it. You decide.

The Tao Te Ching tells us that the Tao, or the way or path, is "the deep source of everything. It is nothing and yet everything." Taoists believe that if one ignores divine wisdom that tells us not to suffer, not to struggle against the oneness of life by not following the intrinsic intelligence of nature itself, then one cannot know the ways of wisdom. Living with Tao, one has wisdom and will live in harmony. Nevermind the yin and yang of it.

The Jewish people listen to their own form of wisdom found in the Torah, which says, "Obey my voice, and I will be your God, and you shall be my people; and walk in all the way that I command you, that it may be well with you." In other words, listen to the wisdom of God and even your bagels will refrain from spoiling.

Islam says, "There is no god but God, and Muhammad is the Prophet of God." Incidentally, Islam means peace, and that's one factor the news always seems to leave out about the Muslims. I think it's intentional negative propaganda and it needs to stop. Muslims truly believe in peace and they live for peace because a Muslim is "one who submits to God." There's that word again, "God." Are you beginning to see a pattern? Muslims believe that by submitting to God, or Allah, everyone can come together through peace. And by the way, this God sent messengers down to Earth also, and the last messenger to deliver the great, divine wisdom was the Prophet Muhammad. Evidently people everywhere have been hearing God's voice forever and not just the Christians.

Speaking of Christians, they too believe in one God who created the universe and human beings in order to have a relationship with them through various displays of wrath and fury which He knew we would find endearing. This particular God's "messenger" was a bohemian poet named Jesus who really knew how to muck things up. You see, Jesus actually cared about your feelings and was not solely concerned with a bunch of rules set in stone (no pun intended) especially when they couldn't even be read by the illiterate slave people in the first place. (Someone needs to write: "Commandments by Proxy: Don't Write 'Em If They Can't Read 'Em"). Anyway, Jesus left behind a life-changing philosophy of "being," a couple of Broadway musicals, even a Testament of his teachings which is always an annual best-seller. At the time of this writing, Jesus even had a website at: www.jesus.com. And what about the website the Christain church does not want you to read? I dare you to look at this, that is, if you have the eyes to see and ears to hear: http://www.cygnus-study.com/pagecon.shtml.

Now then, the Hindus believe that the "one God" takes on many different forms or aspects. Hindus do not have many gods, but one — despite what a lot of ignorant literature states, calling Hinduism some kind of evil cult of Satan worshippers. It is not. It was one of the very first (if not the first) forms of monotheism, or belief in one god. There is nothing evil or immoral about Hinduism or monotheism, especially when everyone is referring to the same, one God.

The Egyptians also believed in one god who had many aspects or faces depending on his mood, depending on whether He would suddenly become duplicitous and destroy Egyptians in order to benefit the Israelites and the entire Christian religion; not to mention the publishers of the New International Version of the King James Bible and rogue television evangelists now in prison. But I digress...

Okay, so we have a pattern here: messengers from God delivering wisdom to the peoples of the planet. Not bad, not bad at all. Do you think it was the first form of network marketing? What was the reason for spreading all this wisdom around in a thousand different forms? It was to elevate humankind, to enlighten us, to lead the human family to spiritual maturity. In short, divine messengers were sent and people were inspired to write down what they "heard" from a higher power in order to bring us together through wisdom. This is the goal of all wisdom, all religions, all spiritual paths, all higher teachings. We live in a cosmic classroom called Earth. It is our celestial university. Did you realize that the word university does not just mean "college" or formal education? It has a much broader meaning, one that universities all over the world are attempting to instill in their students as they learn from a wide range of knowledge. The grander meaning of university is "a unity of diversities." Earth is humankind's lesson, opportunity, and quest for learning to live with a unity of diversities.

It seems that all the various forms of wisdom come from the same Source. Throughout all the different paths that same Source is known as the one God, or Creator, or Life, or the Divine Intelligence. All these terms and names share the same meaning because they are all talking about the same Source. Different names, same content. Calm down if you're confused, the captain has officially turned off the fasten-seat-belt sign, so feel free to wander throughout the book. Smoking the pages is strictly prohibited, however, and tampering with the pages in any way is a violation of some rule someplace, I'm almost sure of it. But if you're stuck in Siberia, need a good fire to keep from freezing to death, and are still confused anyway, then the only wise thing a student of wisdom *should* do is to quit reading this pulp right now, light it up, and stop interrupting the general flow of my logic here. Now where was I? Ah yes. Oneness.

The source is the "One," just as some scriptures say there is only one God. The ways to describe this "one God" are many. God, or the ultimate Source, is the Truth. And we all know enough at this point in time to know that the truth is true, right? The truth is real. Therefore, one could say that the truth is one and the paths to it are many. That's the way it is whether you like it or not, whether you believe it or not. This book is not about beliefs. It is about wisdom, a way that points towards the truth.

Inside you will find different insights about the truth from people all throughout history from all over the globe. In case you didn't know it, we all live on the same planet and we all breathe from the same atmosphere. Are you getting my drift? While this book is about sharing, it is also about breaking down the stupid walls and barriers to the truth. It is about exploding some of the hideous myths handed down from history. It is about celebrating life, itself. It is about seeing the person in front of you as nothing but another human being who wants and needs love — the highest wisdom. Indeed, Baha'u'llah seemed enlightened enough to be a modern global businessman, didn't he? Perhaps he would work for Arthur Anderson's "One World. One Organization." Yeah. He was a wise man of vision.

Wisdom deals with the truth while beliefs deal with what thoughts a person thinks. Haven't you ever "believed" in something that never transpired or that simply wasn't true? Most people have done this. I even did this with a few people I dated. Mere belief is not enough, and you knew that before you read this book. While your belief may be an error in your perception about reality, the error itself has no effect on reality. Why? Because when we think of something and then project it onto the world, we are seeing something that isn't there. We just *believe* it's there, we just *hope* it's there, we just *pray* that it's there. All this believing, hoping, and praying doesn't make something true in reality. Nevertheless, our world is run by opinions, thought systems, ideas, and beliefs.

"So what?" you say.

I say, "Wake up people, *and smell the audit!*"

Each one of the "messengers" who wrote divine, inspired words of God founded a specific religion of the world. As we know, there are literally thousands of different forms of religion. However, all of them deal with the same content despite the different forms. That content is what is universally known as God. From this divine source of everything comes wisdom. Every single religion on the planet has different rituals, prayers, mantras, and traditions by which its people can pay homage to and worship God. For every person on Earth there are an equal number of different perceptions of God because each of us sees the world and the universe differently. This is a fact.

Think of wisdom as the center of a wheel. All the spokes extending from the wheel's center are all the different forms of God's wisdom expressed in various languages, bibles, holy places, inspired writings, churches, universities, ministers, gurus, counselors, therapists, scientists, world leaders, saints, martyrs, kings, queens, presidents, managers, CEOs, teachers, and mentors throughout the entire world.

While all the spokes appear different externally, they all lead back to the same internal content: the One, the Unity, the Universal Intelligence, the Divine God. It doesn't matter what we call the spokes, or different forms of expression. Unfortunately, that is exactly what people have focused on: differences. I find it amazing that people would rather focus on what keeps us apart rather than what can bring us together. It's a shame that some people have to die off before the rest of us are allowed to have a little more peace. Some people insist on treating others as if they are separate from this planet and their seeking salvation in separation is not a good idea for practicing love in the world.

Why? Because it is a way of seeing the world in separate parts and not seeing the oneness and wholeness of life. This is mankind's biggest error in perception and it needs correction. All parts lead back to the whole, the one, God. That is all that the word wisdom or God means: the entirety of the universe. And the last time I checked, no one human being has the power to separate *anyone* from the whole of life. No one has the power to remove the spokes of the wheel because no one has the power to destroy what life and the universe have created. I have met a lot of people who believe this is possible, though, and justify the exclusion of certain "types" of people from the whole of life – as if that were humanly possible. This idea of separation is downright ridiculous because it deals not with reality and truth but the thoughts, feelings, perceptions, and beliefs of people. These are faces of False Evidences Appearing Real, or FEAR.

From Baha'u'llah's statement about "the Earth is but one country and mankind its citizens" you can see the visionary wisdom this man had. He looked at the oneness of the peoples of our planet and saw not differences and separation, but the wholeness of life. After all, it is life that creates us not the government, not the job or career, not some religion or belief system, not some dream in your head. You did not create yourself. Life did. To say that life is holy means that life is *whole*. Baha'u'llah saw harmony and unity, not separation and discord. He spoke of inclusion, not exclusion. He saw life full of love not hate. Love creates while hate destroys. But what does hate destroy? Hate destroys *love*, got it? And when you hate someone or something, it's not that you're only harming others. You are harming yourself, first. You are denying the power of life, which is the power of love and joy and ultimately wisdom, itself. In short, you are not honoring God's creation because let's face it: if there is the one God that created everything, that means God created EVERYTHING and EVERYONE! Love, the highest form of God's wisdom, is for everyone, everywhere, no exceptions. Period!

It reminds me of the scientific axiom about the law of conservation of energy in the universe: "Energy can neither be created nor destroyed although it can change form." We are one, together, and we share a common set of feelings, beliefs, values, desires, hopes, dreams, nightmares, and fears. We are one people. One planet. One energy. One.

These are facts that go beyond the mere words of a belief system. These statements are true whether we believe them or not, whether we like them or not. Reality deals with facts. Not beliefs. And it certainly does not deal with anyone's precious, over-protected opinions about what they would rather have reality be. The book called "A Course in Miracles" states at one point:

"Do not ascribe to your brother a role that you imagine would bring happiness to you, and do not try to hurt him when he fails to take the part that you assigned to him in what you dream your life was meant to be."

Because people have recorded their thoughts in historical documents, journals, inspired writings, secret letters, poetry, books, manuscripts, even on papyrus paper, we have a written record of what goes on inside the hearts and minds of human beings. And while those records look, sound, and feel different, their core essence is still the same.

The thoughts and ideas that lie behind the physical words and language are what is important. This core essence is what I call *content* while the sentence or language used to express a particular thought, idea, belief, or inspiration is what I call the *form* of that content. Wisdom comes in as many different forms as there are atoms, neutrons, and neutrinos. No one atom is more special than another, no one person is more special than another. Get my drift? No one atom can be destroyed and taken out of this universe. When we can do that, this book will be entirely obsolete and so will all worldly religions. But for now, we have wisdom to teach us how to either destroy reality as we know it, or create a better one. It's up to you. It's up to all of us.

The mental "technology" already exists (the brain), along with a few thousand years of research (wisdom), for us to end the problems running our lives. Violence is not "out there" in the world. It is inside our minds, first, and then it is projected onto the world where we react to it. In essence, we are reacting to images that we have made up, which means we are reacting to something that is not really out there. This is insanity and we need to rid ourselves of this cycle.

Difficulty arises when we want to escape the violent thoughts we all have that say we are not good enough, smart enough, rich enough, cool enough, all that stuff. All our money cannot buy peace of mind, let alone world peace. All our religion merely sustains an ancient status quo that declares one religion is better than another and is therefore "right." Reward and punishment has ruled the world for thousands of years. Jesus has not returned yet, and I don't blame Him. We have a long way to go. And we have no one else to point the finger at but ourselves. Each one of us is responsible for the current condition of the world. Each one of us holds in trust our own mental technology. Each one of us must be responsible with it. Each one of us will be held responsible for creating more peace…or more war. What do *you* want? What would you rather have?

Peace, in actuality, is only a decision away. But we have too much to do. We have to go shopping, we have to go to work, we have to do our homework, we have to go to the movies, we have to diet, we have to clean the house, we have to pray, we have to do so many things EXCEPT be *the* examples of loving, non-violent, peaceful human beings. We are human beings first—citizens, CEOs, managers, laborers, teachers, students, and clergymen second. We need to be human beings who realize the fragility of human life. We need to be human beings who can see the innocence in the person in front of us. We need to serve one another instead of putting each other down, making snide jokes, hoping that someone will pay attention to our boring monotonous chatter that has ruled our minds for the last several thousand years.

A lot of vicious chatter goes on inside our heads, which provokes us to act upon it in the world. Except we never want to appear as vicious as our thoughts, so we alter the *form* of our actions. The content of our thoughts still consists of nonloving, fearful thoughts. It is almost as if we have conspired to destroy the world *politely*.

We have so many knowings, opinions, wantings, and prejudices but very little peace of mind. Why? In addition, why do we demand that our children respect us—

when we do not even respect each other as adults? The fact is, we often treat each other very badly. If we see anything in another person other than just another human being trying to find some joy in his life, then perhaps we should be the person to GIVE IT to him.

In doing so, we will find the meaning of life. Our function is to make life beautiful not only for ourselves but for others, too. Our function is to make other people happy, make ourselves happy, and to live and love in peace. Some people want to know the meaning of life. Well, is that enough "meaning" for you?

You be the one to bring a little peace into someone's life. Nothing is more sacred than that. Nothing is more important than healing the world. Nothing would please God more than for all of us to get along, once and for all. Even if you don't believe in God, don't you think world peace sounds more interesting than the next episode of "Who Wants to be a Millionaire?" If you don't, you might be part of the problem. As long as we can relax without neglecting someone who needs us I think whatever people do in their personal time is fine. Don't get me wrong, here. I'm not the free-time police.

And speaking of neglect...

Part of the violence each one of us contributes to on a very small, almost microscopic level each day (in this country, at least) is that of ignoring what is really important. Anymore it seems that some people no longer know what they need, much less want. So they binge on sensationalism: the two-sided, ever-spinning coin of pleasure and pain. Where is peace?

Our culture lives for entertainment—as if anyone

could be so bored! Our culture excuses "just getting by" in school—as if anyone desires to play small on the global stage by not studying or performing up to his potential in school. Our culture politely ignores coming down to a sub-level by taking some alcohol on a joy ride through our veins so we have no idea what reality is anymore. We thrive on stimulation—some people find it in violence, others find it in sex, drugs, alcohol, gambling, crime, or even bad food that does nothing for our bodies but makes them fatter, sicker, and more clogged up with mucus and toxins. No wonder we are physically and psychically depressed! So why are we perplexed by all the heart attacks, depression, suicide, AIDS, cancer, STDs, or even the common cold?

We could say that we are more dis-eased now than ever before. People live longer, but they are more depressed at the seeming meaninglessness of life. People live longer but their money runs out, and so does family support, family concern, family love. Everything is in constant change and it is up to us to get a hold of ourselves and just STOP and REALIZE:

How long does it take to commit to the obvious:
we are not at peace??!!

The world will not change until we change. Gandhi said, "Be the change you want to see in the world." We need to end the violence inside our minds first and then the world will seem to take care of itself. If we can stop wanting to be right about our opinions and focus instead on being happy, all of us will be much better off in the long run. Would *you* rather be right, or would *you* rather be happy? Someone once told me that success is getting what you want while happiness is wanting what you get. Does that fit your life?

A lifestyle of peace demands that we actually *be peaceful.* That means we cannot go around pointing the finger at other people to do it. We cannot go around blaming other people either—who knows what they are going through anyway? Maybe their mom just died—*you have no idea.* Just butt out! Offer peace instead of nagging criticism. It is still loving. It is still the "right" thing to do, and people love it. Who doesn't love peace? Can you see someone's fear, bad hair day, or manic Monday as a call for wisdom? Maybe you should help them.

Our obsession with ourselves, at the expense of other people, means that our perfectionism and narcissism of the last millennium has to end or peace will never happen. It just won't! We can *only* work on ourselves—we cannot change our neighbor. We need to concentrate on being the type of man or woman God, or the Universe, or our own higher mind would have us be.

This demands a lifestyle adjustment: you have to LIVE in peace, not just talk about doing it. The next era is about actualizing the words we have been saying all along. The next phase of human consciousness is about "follow-through." The next age is about putting it all together, *using* all the techniques, *applying* the lessons of life to life itself.

Your life is not an idea in your head! It is very real! What you perceive your life to be may be called your "perception" of it. But the fact remains: if you are reading these words, YOU ARE ALIVE! The question is, now what?! How do you want to live your life? Who are you? What do you want? Where are you going? Why are you here? The 20th Century was mostly about talk. Now, we have to do the walk. So start walking! Peace is only *steps* away, but you have to take the fist step. *You* have to take the first step. Get walking!

Peace requires that we DO IT, not just talk about it.

Do we want the next millennium to be the age of cultural peace or just more of the same—WAR? What do *you* want it to be? What are you doing about it? First, start with yourself. That is the only responsibility we *can* have. If each person saved himself from the violence in his own mind this world could be changed so fast. You have no idea! If everybody just focused on the little compromises he made with peace and turned that around, we could see a dramatic change. We could be the example for the rest of the world; and believe me, they're watching.

One of the roadblocks to realizing peace in the world, on a global scale, is the roadblock of "thinking." Our opinions get us into more trouble than not, don't they? Mine do. All of us have opinions and prejudices. These are part of the roadblock called "thinking." Thoughts get in the way. Then we think that just because we are having a thought (which is only in our head) then that "thought" must be the way things really are. This is wrong. This is the problem.

Thoughts are only our perception of the world. We see only what we want to see. We see only with our eyes, not with our hearts. We listen only to our limited opinions, not to our deeper conscience. We never consciously intend to hurt anybody. But that is not the problem.

The problem is that *we never consciously intend to love anybody.* Who actually wakes up everyday actively hating people? We may not call it "hate" but that may be how our behavior appears to others with whom we interact. It is not their responsibility to re-interpret our bad behavior. It is up to each one of us to start behaving well. We need to increase our awareness of the person standing in front of us and show her mercy.

Now then. How many of you actively love people — which means *really focusing on* bringing more peace into the world? Most of us would rather just voice our opinions. Opinions are for sale in our country because everything is commercialized. There is no way out of it. Not yet.

Religion is one area in particular in which all of us have very strong opinions invested. Opinions are still just that: opinions. They are nothing more than the thoughts in our heads. For every person on the planet there are an equal number of opinions about God. So why can't we just respect everybody's opinion and just *get on with it?!* Because some people do not want to change. They are perfectly happy believing they are absolutely right (at the expense of others), while everyone else is completely wrong. Talk about arrogance.

Again, I ask you: would you rather be right, or would you rather be happy? What do you think peace is, anyway? Is it that *your opinion is Absolute?* I don't think so. A little more is demanded of you. A little more honesty is needed. A little more respect and dignity shown to others is demanded from you.

Because religion is such an emotionally-charged subject we need to be gentle with it. We need to treat it carefully as we move toward the truth. You know that saying about "The truth hurts?" It's wrong. Truth doesn't hurt. Moving out of your comfort zone may be uncomfortable, but once you get to the truth it's great, it's beautiful, and you'll love it. It's better than... chocolate. Usually.

Religious discussions often evoke strong feelings. It is true that feelings do exist. However, they are only your feelings *about* religion. In no way can an opinion threaten anything real. Fearful thoughts about religion are nothing more than fearful thoughts. They are not necessarily *real because all fear is a projection.*

This doesn't mean your feelings don't get hurt, but it does mean that you do not have to choose to feel that way *any more*. Instead, you can choose to be at peace. You could say there is no "religion" in the world, but there is a state of being that is religious. True religion is all about peace on earth, not about having a war over whose religion is "right" and whose is "wrong."

Those wars are over mere opinions. Opinions are not real in the sense that they cannot be eternal. Opinions change, they are not forever. Opinions are not of the mind of God, of eternal wisdom, because only God and true wisdom are eternal.

God is not concerned with your opinions. God is concerned only with what is real. Peace is real. Being religious is also real. It is time that the religions of the world focused on being happy—being at peace— rather than being "right." I am almost *sure* God would approve. What do you think? Perhaps you should find out.

That is what this book is for. It is to show you that all world religions are merely saying the same things. All world scriptures were transcribed in the language that was right for their people, or culture. Some are in Sanskrit, some are in Hebrew, some are in Chinese, some are in Arabic, some are in English. God has spoken all over the globe, you know, not just to the Pope! God certainly has been doing a lot of talking over the last 2000 years. Inside you will find God speaking through holy scriptures and also through people doing holy things. Inside this book is what God has had to say... to *all* of us.

We probably have an opinion about what we think a holy person looks like, acts like, talks like, and so on. That does not make our opinion about holy people *real*, in the sense that holy people do not manifest only according to our personal views. A holy person does not care what you think about him because a holy person is a *whole person* – he does not need your opinion in order to function, in order to get on with life. Your vote, your say, your opinion is irrelevant because the holy person does not necessarily follow *your* word. He follows *God's* word—and God's word cannot be commercialized. It cannot be "owned" by anyone, by any group, by any one religion or spiritual path or master.

Wisdom is always direct, impersonal, and Absolute.

Each one of us has a responsibility for the future of humanity. Each one of us has a special mission. Each one of us is part of the plan for peace. Indeed, each one of us is an example to our children of how to live a productive life and still remember that wisdom means living in peace. We need to pledge to the future that we will not do anything that compromises our responsibility toward realizing world peace. You can still keep your job, you can still keep your fancy clothes. And you do not have to manifest yourself as a nun or a priest. God is not asking you why you are not Mother Teresa—God is asking you why you are not *yourself.*

So who are you, anyway? You are a holy child of God, which simply means you are a sacred creation of the Universe. Holy means "whole." Your opinions are meaningless, yet the essence that is really *You* is the light of the world. Be kind to yourself. Don't undermine yourself, don't exalt yourself. Be peaceful. Peace offends *no one.* Therein lies eternal wisdom.

When you are holy, it does not matter what the outer conditions are like. Your own inner light of holiness will shine through all that anyway. Mother Teresa did not need to wear Chanel suits or drive a sports car. She did more *real* work than most of us. Her work was eternal. She was in contact with loving the human being without judging him as to whether or not he was worthy of love. *Now that is incredible wisdom*! Her work touched people's hearts, she did not go around nagging people. Instead she loved them—there is a difference. I don't think Mother Teresa was waiting to cash in her stock options before she could do the work of God. I do not think Mother Teresa was too concerned with the outer conditions. She had an *inner* fire, a burning desire to love the person in need.

So just start where you are, with what "is." Have a zero tolerance policy for prejudice and discrimination *of any kind.* Practice non-violence and then *do not support anything that is violent.*

Respect the lives of others by not imposing your free will on someone else's free will—remember that it is called "free" for a reason (hint: your name, your ownership, your "vote" has nothing to do with it!).

Protect the sacredness of vulnerability by *allowing time* for people, love, and peace to *blossom in life.* Peace cannot be bought at the store in just ten minutes. Peace takes time—*that is the only true function of time in the first place.*

Share your time with others—have genuine sincerity without excluding others. Sharing peace involves *inclusion.* Exclusion causes wars. Never undermine another human being—*defend freedom in terms of its content, not its form. The content of true freedom leads to peace.*

Support and promote healthy ways to communicate while allowing the other person to maintain a sense of self-esteem and dignity.

Respect all forms of life—*peace demands living in harmony with what God created and not always fighting against it.* Help contribute to the development of peaceful communities— *demand that peace be shared equally with everyone, everywhere.* These are some of the responsibilities the new era demands from us, *by* us—the human beings who are citizens of this not-yet united world. *We the people* can do this. *We the people* can bring an end to the history of war because we desire peace. *We the people* are ready to welcome a new way of looking at the world using a thought system based on love rather than fear. *We the people* deserve peace on earth, goodwill toward all men, women, and children. *We the people* need to stop waiting for God to fix the world's problems. God is waiting for *we the people* to fix the world's problems. We *can* do it. We *must* do it. And we *will* do it. After all, our "will" is all we have… *and it's free!*

Gods
and
Spiritual
Paths

Gods and Spiritual Paths

GODS HAVE SPOKEN to mankind throughout history. Divine wisdom has lead entire dynasties, nations, and cultures to their greatest successes. Some have fallen to the lowest depths of despair, while still others have faced nothing less than their own extinction. Clearly the wisdom of the gods has been extremely powerful. Peace will reign or war will wage. Either way, our destiny seems to be "up to the gods." Or is it? Why are more people *not* flocking to churches by the millions to discover for themselves the "peace of God that passeth all understanding?"

Why are the best and the brightest moving in mass exodus toward Eastern religions, alternative spiritualities, or new age organizations? Why are more people waking up to a balanced thought system of wisdom that uses *both* the rational left brain and the emotional right brain when it comes to religion, spirituality, and wisdom? Why must faith crumble when we apply thinking and reasoning to it? These are big questions, yet wisdom demands a questioning process if we are to distinguish what is true from what is false. Only then will people flock en masse toward a perception of the ultimate oneness of wisdom and humanity, the one god, the one truth, the one light, and the higher intelligence in order that the followers of this wisdom be "as numerous as the stars in the sky and as the sand on the seashore." (Genesis 22:17) Wisdom is infectious inspiration.

Gods have inspired some to worship peacefully while instructing others to destroy entire cultures. Gods can display both gentleness and wrath. However, after thousands of years we still have not "seen" a god. But lately God seems to be having conversations with a lot of people. Apparently retail has finally figured out what the church has always known: God sells. Yeah, but what *brand* of god do people want nowadays? What *style* of god fits your needs? Does god choose you or do you choose god? If you choose god, which one is the *right* one? Are there more than just the ubiquitous, ontological *one*?

Many names from all over the globe are used to describe the one and only God of the universe: Creator, Tao, Divine Wisdom, Holy Spirit, Christ, Allah, Messiah, Almighty, Him, Her, Ahura Mazda, Lord of Wisdom, Krishna, Shiva, Brahman, Nameless One, Formless One, Buddha, Paramatman, Universal Intelligence, Zen, Nzame, Mu'umba, Chineke, Ngai, Imana, Opu Tamuno, Great Mother, Source of All Being, Great Providence, Spirit, Yaweh, Jehovah, Adonai, Elohim, Hashem, Shaddai,

Shekhinah, Love, Holy Spirit, The Man Upstairs, even Ama-ama-amasi-amasi from the Igbo regions of Africa which means "He Who Is Never Fully Known."

In the Ojibwa language of the Algonquin Native American Indians the totality of spiritual forces is called "K'che Manitou." In Japanese Shinto the name of God is "Tsukihi" which means Sun and Moon. The Rastafarians, or Rastas, use the term "I and I" rather than "you and I" in their conversations because they believe that all people are equal, bound together by the one god, Jah. In addition to all the internationally different names for the "One" God, there are also some interesting interpretations of God's divine wisdom.

For the Rastafarians, Ganja – otherwise known as marijuana – is used for religious purposes. They cite its use in the Bible in Psalms 104:14. It says, "He causeth the grass for the cattle and herb for the service of man." Apparently Ganja is used for treating the common cold and the flu. Other names for Ganja are Iley, callie, and holy herb. They also cite its use in:

Genesis 3:18, "…thou shalt eat the herb of the field."

Exodus 10:12, "…eat every herb of the land."

Proverbs 15:17, "Better is a dinner of herb where love is, than a stalled ox and hatred therewith."

You can see how interpretations of the so-called "inspired" word are just that: interpretations. Of course, with the regular use of Ganja all your words can be "inspired" or at least very deep and profound, right? We won't even get into whether or not people actually saw miracles or mere hallucinations from using the "holy herb."

Interpretations about the inspired Word cannot be absolute or even literal "translations" of the one God because all languages can only *describe* reality. Language interprets our thoughts, albeit in a rather clunky manner at times. Language is descriptive, not literal. Most importantly, language is relative and does more to bind us together than push us apart. The fact that we all use language is so universal, prima facie, that to see or hear differences in one another just because of a different language (i.e.: different form of religion, different names for the one God) is downright ignorant.

That is why religious fundamentalism's regard for the word of God being "literal" is so silly. Yet most people believe their religion and their god are somehow special to them and they are not universal in terms of their content. This is stupid. Famous language expert Steven Pinker is one of the world's leading experts on language and the mind. He is the director of the Center for Cognitive Neuroscience at MIT and recognizes how even languages from all over the world are much more similar than not. In his book, "The Language Instinct," he states, "Knowing about the ubiquity of complex language across individuals and cultures and the single mental design underlying them all, no speech seems foreign to me, even when I cannot understand a word...I imagine seeing through the rhythms to the structures underneath, and sense that we all have the same minds."

Thus explodeth the Tower of Babel myth. As far as

that goes, how about exploding the even bigger myth that Christianity is the only way to know God? How about it, people? If anything stresses the differences more than the unity of mankind, I c an't think of a better example than the modern church – which is anything but modern. Chuck Meyer, Vice President of Operations and Chaplain at St. David's Medical Center in Austin, Texas, states, "The institutional Church we know so well is dying. In fact, it may already be dead. Its structure and theology make no sense today, and haven't for decades." I agree. The church has lost sight of wisdom, choosing dogmatic drama instead. Without wisdom there can be no love and without love there can be no unity, no harmony, no intelligence, and the eradication of the myth that we are all different at our core.

There aren't even any differences at the core level of what language is all about, at the level of its basic, human, universal content. We are of one mind, in content, although that one mind expresses itself in many different forms. And you knew that before you read this book!

Slowly but surely we are starting to see this oneness in humanity. It's about time! How long does it take to commit to the obvious, people?! We are finally beginning to recognize the reality that we live in a global civilization. We are beginning to think and reason with wisdom. Wisdom has the power to shed light on darkness, and bring wholeness back to our awareness ending our perceptions about differences and the alleged "separations" between people.

Cultures and people are no longer "separated" by vast expanses of land, or great walls built around a country or even a castle. Technology has removed all the barriers preventing separation between the peoples of this world. The only thing that separates us now is our belief about the other person. We still feel threatened by what we do not readily understand, much less know. We still live under tribal systems of "stay with your own group" and "never deviate from the group" mainly because the group's survival once depended upon those rules. Not anymore, though. Survival in those days meant just that: *surviving life*. We have moved beyond this lower level of existence by becoming interested in the quality of life. We want meaning, depth, joy, health, abundance, love, and serenity.

Nowadays it's possible to survive with nothing more than the designer clothes in our closets, yellow SUVs, organic foods in our SubZeros, and our trusty arsenal of credit cards ready for action at the slightest craving for a latte. The form of survival has changed, but not the content of it. Deep down we still believe that "death" will result if we walk a path very different from our own. But why?

We would not literally die, but our illusions about what we believe would experience a sort of death. It is that death that we are unconsciously aware of at all times. And it is that death that scares us to such a degree that we will do whatever is necessary to defend our belief systems, our opinions, our preferences, our likes and dislikes. We will protect to the death (a major detriment to progress) our own thoughts because we are the thinker of those thoughts. We made them. Our thoughts, beliefs, and opinions seem to *literally* embody our perceptions and ideas about our Selves, friends, neighbors, family, work, and everything in our world. If that perception is brought to disillusionment, it shatters and we "die."

We are becoming more comfortable with the fact that living in a global civilization means it is imperative we not only respect and to some degree understand one another, but also live together...in peace. At last we have begun to realize the **fact** that at the root of **all** world religions is humanity's search for the Meaning of Life, or God, or The Creator, or Reality. It does not matter what form of a name we give it. The content is identical. In the peace of wisdom there are no conflicts, no differences. The Truth is one and the paths to it are many.

The truth is true no matter who says it, writes it, preaches it, or follows it. Only the truth is real. Everything else is an illusion of our misperceptions, prejudices, grudges, beliefs, misinformation, wantings, knowings, desires, and even our religions. Luckily we are sophisticated enough by now to recognize that the principles of the truth can be translated into many thousands of different *forms*, but the *content* of the truth remains the same. Form will always change, but truth's content stays the same. Like wisdom, truth is eternal.

In this age of rapid change, there is a lot of debate about whether or not corporations will someday rule the world. If they do, it will be a small kingdom in comparison to the empire we have constructed based on our belief systems and our world religions. Indeed, corporations and global financial markets may be closing the gap on who will monitor and control the circulation of capital, goods, services, and information. But under what guidance, credo, rules, norms, and laws does anyone do anything? What are the motivating factors that influence such strong changes in a society?

The answer is simple: belief systems. Now that we know that, where do we go? Like in the world of Star Trek, in which a futuristic culture is based on the "Prime Directive" of non-interference, let us "speculate" the outcome based on current conditions (no previous knowledge of Vulcan logic is required). Business has aspirations of greater and greater profit, increased efficiency and speed, and low costs. Our current capitalistic system is totally dependent upon the manmade "laws" of supply and demand. As an aside, they have nothing to do with the eternal laws of cause and effect, but that's a different book altogether.

Look at how our economy works. As long as we buy a particular thing, it will be sold. Many of us stopped buying the cheapest coffee at the grocery store after we discovered that Starbucks is better. So now business is jumping on the bandwagon by making any little adjustments needed in order to compete with top-selling brand name coffees. And if you want to sleep at night, all is not lost because now business can afford to make it decaffeinated. If you are eco-friendly, you buy decaf that is Swiss Water Processed rather than chemically treated (don't worry about the chemicals, though. The roasting temperature is so high that all the chemicals burn off leaving no residue. As a former Starbucks manager, I had to know that.) If all of us stopped buying coffee, it would no longer be sold *anywhere.* When the demand stops, prices go up, the bank goes ballistic, and businesses have serious brainstorming to do if they want to stay profitable!

If there is anything consumers do not want—for whatever reason—all they have to do is stop buying it. Vote with your dollars! But we no longer know **why** we buy anything anymore. We are caught in a stream of unconsciousness, like numb and dumb robots who merely **react** to the advertising, propaganda, and opinions of the media and the world of capitalism. We consume products, services, and information but we can no longer digest it. Something unique is occurring in the United States, though. We are becoming disillusioned, realizing the folly of attempting to find love in weight-loss products, gym equipment, or that perennial favorite of most men—the new car.

Most of what we buy is junk. Most of what we believe in is mere opinion and not truth or fact. Most everything we accumulate or think about is filler, "like something we wade through on the way to some Heaven," says Marianne Williamson. Most of our excess is unnecessary simply because we **do not need it!**

This does not mean you have to sell everything you own, never make another purchase in your life, or manifest as the Dalai Lama. It only means that you become totally honest with yourself. See the fact as a fact. See beyond the illusions. If you are an engineer, then you are an engineer—but you will not build anything that does not meet a need. If you are a teacher, then you are a teacher—but you will not teach anything that is false. And if you're an insurance agent, you're in my prayers. God bless you — for you know not what you do, evidently.

It is unfortunate, in some ways, that we have moved

away from our original agrarian society. For the most part, citizens were self-sufficient. Not because they chose to be, but because they had to be independent in order to survive. People had their own land, fresh air, fresh food, and regular daily exercise just from walking and working the land. People in communities were closer to each other emotionally than they are today. They understood that independence also meant *interdependence* as in sharing and being cooperative. Back then outlaws would occasionally ride through town and shoot people, yes. But today kids attend school and get shot by their ex-boyfriend or some other smooth criminal who is full of nothing but fear, insecurity, and ignorance – an ignorance about the oneness of life. When we harm anyone, anywhere, at any time (including ourselves) then we have given in to temptation. Who has the wisdom today not to give in to temptation? How many parents blow this in front of their kids? How many kids blow it? How many people in government blow it? Temptation is easy. The freedom that comes from discipline is not particularly difficult. To a lot of people, discipline – especially spiritual discipline – is apt to be more personally insulting than anything else. That's because wisdom demands that you let go of all that is not authentically you. Unfortunately we tend to let go of wisdom before we let go of our prejudices, bad mental habits, and other problems.

When there is a lack of wisdom the world becomes a very dangerous place. Intelligence dies. Ignorance spreads. It's not a mystery why we have become so dependent upon the externals for security and self-esteem. We chose to overlook our own vulnerability.

The death of a lifestyle that afforded us self-sufficiency and simplicity (now all the rage) means that we have allowed a shift toward total dependency. We believe and feel that we are so helpless, lonely, weak, poor, depressed, undereducated, underpaid, underappreciated, and co-dependent to such a degree that we are caught in a massive delusion of our own making. It is similar to the movie *The Matrix*, which paints an even more grotesque picture of reality than the one discussed here. It is reminiscent of George Orwell's *Animal Farm* and *1984*. How long will we remain dependent upon our self-made delusions of time, space, credit card bills, and the disease to please? The disease to please applies not only to our relationships with people, but it also applies to our relationship with God. We have made ourselves sick to death (literally) over this one. Had you noticed?

Today, in the "Zen and now" of it all, look at our world and see what we have done to it. Some things are irreparably bad while other things are undeniably good. Intolerance, killing, hate, and war are bad. Vaccination, disease control, compassion, and literacy are good. We are living in a new era of moral responsibility for the information we use.

Are you ready to experience the age of e-wisdom?

We use information all the time, but how wisely do we use it and at what expense? As we near the close of the frenetic newness of information age (it was only a blip anyway, right?) we need to start asking **how** we use information and **why** we are using it in the first place. We need to seriously think about the ramifications of ignoring other belief systems which help to shape and mold the peoples of this planet. This planet is not yet connected in its beliefs and values, but it is connected by the internet which has within it a spiritual universe all its own, as you will find out later on in the book.

We have delved into our own self-induced crises and darkness long enough now, thinking that if only we could understand the bad stuff it would go away. Oprah talks about the "disease to please" – it seems that the flip side of the classic, passive victim is now the active one who tries to meet everyone else's needs before her own. If only we could understand or help the other person then we could control situations better. However, the problem lies not in the effects we experience in situations. The problem lies in who causes the effects in the first place.

Should we please ourselves first before we attempt to please others? But isn't it true that we have to please others before we can please ourselves? Where do we begin?! Waaah!

Well, c'mon folks! Aren't there enough hours in the day? Obviously we have to work on BOTH!

The fact remains: because we feel so out of control we compensate by wanting to control everything and everyone in sight. In doing so, we blatantly show our arrogance. We think we *can* know everything and we have this need to control everything. If we do not control everything, we become afraid that we will end up being the poor shlep who wore shlumpy clothes and died a shmo. History proves us wrong, though. We do not need to control everything. History and wisdom prove that at the rate we are going, if all of us were to stay on track with the current business paradigms and the current mindset of religion in the world, we will extinguish ourselves. Business and religion do not currently mix, as the Summer 1999, (volume 40, number 4) report in MIT's Sloan Management Review discovered.

They found out that people talked about wanting to feel more spiritual at work. But when people's actions were monitored, their walk differed from their talk. Vastly. CEOs always seem to crave the next best thing, including corporate religion. What some fail to do with all their soul-stirring rhetoric, however, is implement new ways of looking at situations. MIT stated that this is our new challenge. "We have gone too far in separating key elements. We need to integrate spirituality in management. No organization can survive long without spirituality and soul."

Throughout their study of spirituality in the workplace they noted how most people wanted to express their spirituality at work, but were extremely hesitant to do so. Sadly, it seems that business and religion/spirituality do not mix. Is there a lack of wisdom here? What are businesses and religion doing that keeps them so separate? Is it even correct to say that business and religion do not mix? Do we know **why** they do not mix? Let's find out.

If we continue in the same direction in business, the laws of supply and demand will eat us alive. The population is expanding exponentially around the world. That is an enormous demand to have to supply.

We already know that the supply of jobs does not exist for everyone on this planet to have enough food to eat, water to drink, clothes to wear, and then to be able to buy a house, a car, an education, and still pay the bills. The **majority** of the global population contains an enormous amount, or supply, of mouths to feed whose demand cannot currently be met by the supply of jobs in big business. This is a **fact**.

We absolutely have to turn this around. Money, work, jobs, and business needs to serve **us** instead of us serving **it**. Money has become *the* god. We have made capitalism into an idol. For all the control we secretly desire, we harbor even more anger, self-hatred, and resentment when we recognize the illusion in which we are caught. This is why we cry each time an idol falls.

In his book, "The Crisis of Global Capitalism," George Soros believes that our unquestioning faith in market forces blinds us to current instabilities. Those instabilities have never been addressed and the result has been a chain reaction causing our current crises. It must be from that lack of soul awareness, that disconnection from our higher Selves, or the lack of the oneness of wisdom, right? Well, Soros believes the way out is an open society with an international agenda: "A global society cannot be brought into existence by people or nongovernmental organizations acting on their own....We need such (governmental and public) leadership to form a coalition of like-minded countries committed to the creation of a global open society." Imagine a rich guy like him, an intelligent guy like George touting oneness and like-mindedness. Sounds awfully spiritual, doesn't it? Who do we think made our current crisis in the first place? The government? No.

We are the **only** ones responsible for this because

we made it that way — not God, not the government, not the rest of the plant and animal kingdom. *We the People* did it. Unfortunately, Americans are not the only ones who suffer the problems of our so-called "progress." We create quick-fix solutions so that the problem we solved only creates another problem. Henry David Thoreau saw this in the invention of the steam engine, declaring, "Inherent in it are the seeds for its own destruction."

For all our so-called "control," man is still the only species which consciously undermines itself. No other animal on the face of the planet has instincts that are *as* stupid as some of ours. We have enslaved ourselves to money. It is not even alive, yet we remain trapped by its hold on us.

We bow before a nonliving, nonloving thing. It is like being a drug user: drugs do not care how fast you are moving, they do not care if you are moving too fast. Drugs do not care about you at all, yet some people are seemingly enslaved by them, addicted to them. If drugs are not enough of a trip for them, they turn to something like more money to dull the pain of their own stupidity. Drug addiction and wasting money (not to mention one's life) go hand in hand.

People have died for money. People have lost families over it, divorced because of it, even renounced the hideous world of status quos that demand we be the supply to the religion of capitalism.

What role does religion play in this grand scheme? It tries to pose as the way out. The kind of religion I am talking about here is the one a lot of us call religion, but is not religion at all. This kind of religion has fallen prey to the economics of supply and demand. Instead it uses different names. They are "punishment" and "reward." We have bought what this "religion" has sold for a thousand years. It seems there is no escaping the negative effects of greedy business and its equally devastating twin, fake religion. The two go hand in hand. Look at these comparisons in the following list of examples:

- Whether you like it or not: if you are late for work, you get fired.

- Whether you like it or not: if you do not pay your taxes, you go to jail.

- Whether you like it or not: if you do not "believe" in one particular religion's tribal group dynamics, (say "dogma") then you are free to go to hell.

- Whether you like it or not: if you do not follow the dogma, then you are a heathen, a leech, and a Satan-worshipping sinner (and the fun part is, you still get that glorious never-ending vacation to the hottest spot on earth. Whoopie!).

Traditional business dogma suggests—indeed requires—that we follow supply and demand. Otherwise we must settle for poverty, sickness, weakness, defensiveness, attack, fear, and no Hawaiian retirement. In short: hell.

Religious dogma demands that we continuously, unerringly, and unquestionably supply it with our souls, being fruitful and multiplying all over the place. If we do that, it is no less pernicious than corporations running the world. Look at this seriously for a minute. If everyone on the planet were to "be fruitful and multiply," we would create a huge population explosion, destroying ourselves, because we would use up all the resources. Humans would be breeding like rabbits, all in the name of religious dogma, and eventually swarm the earth like locusts. Scientifically and morally this is dead wrong. Why is that *not* the way to go? Because we would be **dead.** Get it? Businesses cannot meet the demands of survival *already*, so why do we insist on going in the direction which history proves will not work?

I am not against having children or adopting children or anything like that. Nothing could be further from the truth. That is not what I am saying, so do not misquote me or misread this. Please listen.

All I am asking is: how long does it take for us to commit to the obvious? Business and religion need to change their unwavering "dogma" based *not* on truth, but on opinion and belief. If they do not change the way they perceive (and therefore act in the world) they will collapse under the weight of their own short-sightedness and arrogance.

There is a higher road. There is a greater intelligence than the ego-machinations of the greedy, soulless man of business and the repressed, sin-soaked soul of the man of religion. Because we desire such strict rules, because we "need" control over the bottom line of the budget, and because we are obsessed with the "bottom line" of God's sin roster, it seems we face an interesting paradox. The fact that we demand so much control over ourselves, blindly adhere to outdated business paradigms and equally outdated religious prejudices, and cling to obfuscating beliefs, means two things:

1. We actually feel very **out** of control, lost, and soul-less; like we are leading a meaningless life devoid of fulfillment, abundance, pretty skin, enough money; and we do not know **where** we are going or **why.** So we compensate for that lack inside by seeking control. We seek a job because it gives us something to do, something to fill the boredom, something to compensate for our sense that we lack the brains, the body, the education, and sex appeal that everyone else in the world (and in the media) seem to have but we don't.

   The fact that we seek control so much means that our core belief is that we are **out** of control and have no idea how to make decisions on our own, take responsibility for our actions, or cope with our mistakes and successes. Why would we seek control so much if we *knew that we always had it?* Money becomes God, being rich means being immortal, and we can buy happiness if only we knew where to shop.

2. We feel very guilty, sinful, irresponsible, unethi-cal, immoral, mortal, and if we do not "believe" then we do not reap the rewards of heaven and we are punished in hell—where there is no freedom of speech. We keep trying to seek God

which means our core belief is that we are separate from God.

So if our core belief is that we are separate from God, how will we **ever** join with God? We compensate for this lack by following dogma, rituals, ideas, and belief systems. No matter what you believe, it is still under a belief system of thought. They are just ideas in your head. But! It comes down to this: What do we **want** to believe and which way would we **rather** go? We do whatever is necessary to fill up the gap inside, even if it means filling it with what we think God would be like.

Remember Christianity claims that God created us in His image, and not the other way around. So often we project onto God, or the Great Intelligence, our own thoughts, problems, solutions, opinions, and the like. Those are not coming from God at all. Those are suitcases full of our own "stuff." Get rid of them. You have carried them long enough. The brain is very clever, you know. It can make up all kinds of things and stories to evade you. Machinations of the brain are illusions that we need to break down in order to have an **experience** of God rather than just an idea **about** God.

All our rituals, spiritual ambition, and church activities *may* be nothing more than escapism. Only *you* will know the truth about yourself and your beliefs. Look what some people have done to the vast history of religion and religious scriptures, though. It is a nightmare. Scripture becomes commercialized, spirituality "sells," and God needs us to send Him our money so he can continue to broadcast. I do not think Jesus had a Visa, and that's my final answer, Regis.

Being immortal means being as rich as the TV evangelists. All in all, a lot of present-day religion can be chalked up to nothing more than spiritual and religious entertainment. "God" has become big business. We can "buy" God if only we knew the one, right religion, deity, dogma to follow. We have witnessed the biggest marriage in history: Corporation weds Religion in holy matri-money. Fine. But under which religion will the children be baptized?

Never-ending profit (and poverty), according to the business laws of supply and demand, is related to a lot of current religious thought. It is related to religion's never-ending, sinless, immortal salvation according to the present-day dogma of reward and punishment.

Now then... money, by itself, is not evil. Neither is big business. Neither is religion. Religious practice of the principles of the truth (the "spiritual currency" needed for salvation... or at least a good pew close to the altar) is not bad or wrong. That is definitely not what I am saying. It is what we do with it that determines whether or not we are following the principles of the truth or just some habit borne out of routine. We need to start questioning how we use religion and religious thought. We need to think about how we use big business. Do they allow us freedom to do what we want as long as it is truthful, honest, moral, and ethical? Do the avenues of business and religion allow us to act in accord with treating others with respect and dignity? Or do business and religion only meet our own selfish goals and desires, leaving out the rest of the world – which is just another form of separation from the truth, and separation from love?

We are no more liberated from money's grip than we can believe that we are totally guiltless for committing acts that are morally wrong or that go against Absolute Truth. It is imperative that we overcome our fears and our arrogance. They are both lies wasting our valuable time. We could be at peace with our lives instead of shopping for this, praying for that. If you are innocent of guilt, then you live your life! It makes no difference whether you buy more stocks or say more prayers. When you live in Truth, all your actions become holy. Then you do what is necessary, what is needed, what is loving, what is respectful, what is peaceful, and what is responsible.

There is no business higher than the business of living. There is no religion in the world — but there is the religious mind. There cannot be religion in the world because that "world" is still at the level of your perceptions, preferences, opinions, problems, likes, and dislikes. That is **your world**, not the true nature of reality. And you knew that before you read this book, too.

We could all be at peace if we not only wanted it, but actually lived with it. Merely talking about peace does nothing. Talking is just mere words. Merely desiring peace is not enough, either. That is the same as having good intentions. Good intentions are not enough because they are still at the level of your thoughts and not your actions. More is required of us. Otherwise our so-called "intention" of peace is a mystical idea in our heads that allows us to sound very hip in spiritual matters and everyone will think we are "mysterious."

If peace is only a word, then what good is it? What good is meditation and prayer if they are only words or habitual activities? Wanting to be separate from everyone else (posing as pious or ascetic) is still just ambition. Ambition is driven by fear and a lack of love, trust, and faith. It would be better to go out and eat dessert with friends because it's tough to be alone.

Intention means nothing unless you act on it. Good intentions are never enough. Live them! Look at what you are doing with your life. See the fact as a fact, break down the illusions. If you intend to be at peace, then I ask you: "Are you?" Can you stop right now and name every single thing or person that ticks your ticker and honestly say you haven't contributed to the situation in *some* way? We teach people how we want to be treated. What are you teaching others about you?

This reminds of when someone hurts your feelings and they say, "But I never consciously intended to hurt you," or even "I never meant to hurt you." What the heck does that mean? Were they unconscious? The only answer to something like that is: "I know you did not consciously intend to hurt me, but did you consciously intend to love me?" Intentions are not the same as actions. Intentions mean nothing unless they are acted upon.

So, if you only talk about saving money, next time actually SAVE IT. If you only talk about spending more time with your family, but never get around to it, you're making a fool out of yourself. Do you spread joy around instead of condemnation, criticism, and complaints? Spread joy, not your dogma. Share, never teach as if you know and the other person knows nothing. Respect what they have learned in the past. We're not all idiots, you know. Spread some money around like manure, encouraging new things to grow. And always remember that ideas and beliefs are merely ideas and beliefs. They stay that way until you act on them, applying their principles to your life.

And remember that Jesus did not have a VISA card. Neither did Buddha, nor Brahman, nor Lord Shiva. Think about that, atheists, agnostics, and believers alike.

The truth is true whether business practices it or religion performs it. It does not take a person with a Ph.D. from an ivory tower at Stanford or Harvard to write these words and know the truth of them. I know what I am talking about. It does not take a minister, or a preacher, or a priest with a Divinity degree signed by the Pope in order to read these words and discover the truth of them. The wisdom of the truth that is beyond all illusion, all misperception, is still the truth no matter who says it. You cannot deny that, for it is so. History has produced many wonderful business leaders, national champions, spiritual leaders, and religious wisdom. Inside this book are glimpses into this vast area of impeccable wisdom, thought, and dialogue. Please enjoy your reading time always knowing that you are just as innocent as any other soul. You are the light of the world. Let your actions prove it. Let all the celestial wisdom flow right through you.

Now go in peace…
and don't forget to pass it on to somebody else!
Live with Joy.

*My lord,
if I could get
all the wealth
in the world,
would it help me
to go beyond death?*

Maitreyi in the Upanisads

One who gives cools the fire of ambition for wealth.

Yiddish saying

The mechanical faith which depends on authority and wishes to enjoy the conventions of religion without the labor of being religious is quite different from the religious faith which has roots in experience.

Philosopher S. Rodhakrishnan

~

In all worlds He is, the Holy Lord. In darkness He is, light He is. In sun He is, moon He is. Everywhere He is. Everywhere He is. The Lord is in all creation. None knows His coming and going. He is distant. He is near. Multiple He is. One He is. Water, earth, sky, fire and wind, the spark within the body—all these He is. He is the walking jiva here below. Deathless He is.

Rishi Tirumular of the Nandinatha Sampradaya's Kailasa Parampara.

~

*Eye cannot see him, nor words reveal him;
by the senses, austerity, or works he is not
known. When the mind is cleansed by the grace
of wisdom, he is seen by contemplation —
the One without parts.*

Hinduism, Rg Veda 3.54.5

~

*He who looks inwardly at the self
revels in the self;
He who revels in the self
looks inwardly at the self.*

Jainism, Acarangasutra 2.173

~

*We shall show them Our signs on the horizons and
within themselves until it becomes clear to them that
it is the Truth.*

Islam, Qur'an 41.53

~

*For what can be known about God is plain to [all],
because God has showed it to them. Ever since the
creation of the world his invisible nature, namely, his
eternal power and deity, has been clearly perceived in the
things I have been made. So they are without excuse.*

Christianity, Romans 1.19-20

~

A king who can control the urges of his senses will be able to conquer all adversaries.

The Vedas

God is formless. If you think He is big, He is infinite, and if you think He is small, He is infinitesimal.

*Unification Church,
Sun Myung Moon, 10-13-70*

~

*In the beginning was God, Today is God. Tomorrow will be God. Who can make an image of God? He has no body. He is a word which comes out of your mouth.
That word! It is no more,
it is past, and it still lives!
So is God.*

*African Traditional Religions
Pygmy Hymn from Zaire*

~

Invent not similitudes for God; for God knows, and you know not.

Islam, Qur'an 16.74

~

Any and everything and this universe is all the body of God.

Tenrikyo, Ofudesaki 3.40

~

*At this time the World-honored One serenely arose
from meditation and addressed Shariputra:
"The wisdom of all the Buddhas is infinitely
profound and immeasurable. The portal to this
wisdom is difficult to enter. Neither men of
learning nor men of realization are able to
comprehend it.*

Buddhism, Lotus Sutra 2

~

*Beyond the senses is the mind, beyond the mind is the
intellect, higher than the intellect is the great
Atman, higher than the great Atman is the
Unmanifest. Beyond the Unmanifest is the
Person, all-pervading, and imperceptible.*

Hinduism, Katha Upanisad 2.3.7-8

~

*The one that is visible begins from the invisible.
The invisible consists of three ultimates, and
their essence is infinite.*

Korean Religions, Chun Boo Kyung

~

My ancestors stored their money in safes, and I store mine in souls that have been saved, because it is written: The fruit of the righteous is a tree of life, and all who win souls are wise.

Proverbs 11:30

The book of Songs says,
The hawk soars to the heavens above;
Fishes dive to the depths below.
That is to say, there is no place in the highest
heavens above nor in the deepest waters below
where the moral law is not to be found.

Confucianism, Doctrine of the Mean 12

~

Hear O Israel: the Lord our God,
the Lord is One.

Judaism and Christianity Deuteronomy 6.4

~

The sage clasps the Primal Unity,
Testing by it everything under heaven.

Taoism, Tao Te Ching 22

~

There is only one God; all the "gods"
are but His ministering angels who are
His manifestations.

Omoto Kyo, Michi-no-Shiori

~

God is incorporeal, divine, supreme, infinite Mind, Spirit, Soul, Principle, Life, Truth, Love. Science reveals Spirit, Souls, as not in the body, and God as not in man but as reflected by man. The greater cannot be in the lesser... We reason imperfectly from effect to cause, when we conclude that matter is the effect of Spirit; but a priori reasoning shows material existence to be enigmatical. Spirit gives the true mental idea. We cannot interpret Spirit, Mind, through matter. Matter neither sees, hears, nor feels.

Christian Science,
Science and Health, 465,467

~

All things are made to bear record of me, both things which are temporal and things which are spiritual; things which are in the heavens above and things which are on earth, and things which are under the earth, both above and beneath: all things bear record of me.

Church of Jesus Christ of Latter-day Saints, Pearl of Great Price, Moses 6.63

~

Give birth to and nourish all things without desiring to possess them. Give of yourself, without expecting something in return. Assist people, but do not attempt to control them. This how to realize the deep virtue of the universe.

Lao Tzu

The mind which gives life to all the people in the
world: Such is the very mind
which nourishes me!

Shinto, Moritake Arakida
One Hundred Poems about the World

~

Jesus Christ is the same yesterday
and today and forever.

Christianity, Hebrews 13.8

~

The great, unborn Self is undecaying, immortal,
undying, fearless, infinite.

Hinduism
Brihadaranyaka Upanisad 4.4.25

~

Then did I recognize Thee in mind, to be the first
and the last, O Lord.

Zoroastrianism, Avesta, Yasna 31.8

~

*The deeds which I shall do and those which I
have done are now, And the things which are
precious to the eye, through Good Mind, The
light of the sun, the sparkling dawn of the days,
All this is for your praise, O Wise Lord, as
righteousness!*

Zoroastrianism, Avesta, Yasna 50.10

~

*He is the Sole Supreme Being; of eternal
manifestation; Creator, Immanent Reality;
Without fear, Without rancor;
Timeless Form; Unincarnated; Self-Existent;
Realized by the grace of the Holy Preceptor.*

*Sikhism,
Adi Granth, Japuji p.1: The Mul Mantra*

~

*With men it is impossible, but not with God;
for all things are possible with God.*

Christianity, Mark 10.27

~

*You
can
have
anything
as long as
it is not
against
God's
will.*

Yiddish saying

Those who love others only
when others love,
love very small.
Dharma they know not,
nor friendship do they call.
Without perceiving
self-benefit in love,
they do not love at all.

Sri Krishna

The hawk says, "All God did is good."

African Traditional Religions
Ashanti Proverb (Ghana)

~

God is All-gentle to His servants, providing
for whomever He will.

Islam Qur'an 42.19

~

Tao never acts, yet nothing is left undone.

Taoism, Tao Te Ching 37

~

What is God? He/she is an existence that
absolutely lives for others.

Unification Church
Sun Myung Moon, 4-16-88

~

There is no changing the words of God;
that is the mighty triumph.

Islam, Qur'an 10.64

~

God is Love

Christianity, 1 John 4.8

~

My mercy embraces all things.

Islam, Qur'an 7.156

~

The Great Compassionate Heart is the essence of
Buddhahood.

Buddhism, Gandavyuha Sutra

~

To love is to know Me.
My innermost nature,
the truth that I am.

Hinduism, Bhagavad Gita 18.55

~

*There can be no existence
without suffering,
The cause of suffering
is egoistic desire,
The elimination of desire brings
the cessation of suffering,
The way to the elimination
of desire is the
Noble Eightfold Path.*

Buddhism's Four Noble Truths

~

*The Noble Eightfold Path is the
Buddhist scheme of moral and spiritual
self-development leading to Enlightenment:*

1. *Right View*

2. *Right Mental Attitude or Motive*

3. *Right Speech*

4. *Right Action*

5. *Right Pursuits including
   Means of Livelihood*

6. *Right Effort*

7. *Right Mindfulness*

8. *Right Contemplation*

The less effort,
the faster
and more powerful
you will be.

Bruce Lee

~

Never lose
a holy curiosity.

Einstein

~

The intuitive mind will tell the thinking
mind where to look next.

Dr. Jonas Salk

~

Spiritual
Masters
Talk

There is nothing more explosive
than a skilled population
condemned to inaction.
Such a population is likely to become
a hotbed of extremism and intolerance,
and be receptive to any proselytizing
ideology, however absurd and vicious,
which promises vast action.

Eric Hoffer

~

Must then a Christ perish in torment in
every age to save those
that have no imagination?

George Bernard Shaw

~

*Give birth to and nourish all
things without desiring
to possess them.
Give of yourself, without
expecting something in return.
Assist people, but do not
attempt to control them.
This is how to realize the deep
virtue of the universe.*

Lao Tzu

Time is a great legalizer,
even in the field of morals.

H.L. Menchen

~

What the superior man seeks is in himself.
What the mean man seeks is in others.

Confucius

~

A Wounded Deer—leaps highest

Emily Dickenson

~

Doubt is not below knowledge, but above it.

Alain

~

Proclaim liberty
throughout
the land
to all
its inhabitants.

Judaism and Christianity
Leviticus 25.10

~

If you wish to untie a knot,
you must first understand
how it was tied.

Buddhism, Surangama Sutra

~

*One's religion is whatever
he is most interested in.*

J.M. Barrie

~

*The garb of religion is
the best cloak for power.*

William Hazlitt

~

*Nature teaches us to love our friends,
but religion our enemies.*

Thomas Fuller

~

*Reason deceives us more often
than does nature.*

Vauvenargues

~

*Images are more real than anyone
could have supposed*

Susan Sontag

~

*The radical of one century
is the conservative of the next.*

Mark Twain

~

*You have conventions, and the adjusting
of oneself to these conventions is called
thought and action, which is not at all
thought or action, because it is born of fear
and, therefore, cripples the mind.*

Krishnamurti

~

It is possible to respect one person
and not respect another,
but it is not possible
to revere one person
without revering every person.

Gary Zukav

~

Society can be stimulated and let to
embrace dogmas and belief systems.
And we are caught in our nationalistic
views, our religious prejudices.
We have other people making decisions
for us. The result is rather sad.
We have become duty-bound because
we are irresponsible
about our own lives.

Tara Singh

~

*The orthodox also becomes unorthodox
the good also becomes ill.*

Lao Tzu

~

*You are worthy of the name human if you
can practice five things in this world:
respectfulness, magnanimity, truthfulness,
acuity, and generosity.*

Confucius

~

The highest virtue is always against the law.

Emerson

~

*Laws alone cannot secure freedom of
expression; in order that every man present
his views without penalty there must be a
spirit of tolerance in the entire population.*

Einstein

~

Promote the honest over the crooked,
and people will go along.
Promote the crooked over the honest
and people will not obey.

Confucius

~

When faith is insufficient
and there is mistrust,
it is because of
placing too much value
on words.

Lao Tzu

~

Love each other as God loves
each one of you,
with an intense and particular love.
Be kind to each other: It is better to commit
faults with gentleness than to work
miracles with unkindness.

Mother Teresa

~

Ben Azzai used to say:

Do not despise anyone.
Do not regard anything as impossible.
There is no one without his power.
There is no thing without its place

Pirke Avot, IV:3

~

God is within you and every living thing.
Translated, this means that everything living
is a unique representation of God's
identity – mind, spirit, and life.

Iyanla Vanzant

~

Heaven is large,
and affords space
for all modes of
love and fortitude.

Emerson

~

All men who reflect on
controversial matters
should be free from
hatred, friendship,
anger, and pity.

Julius Caesar

~

The unity of freedom
has never relied on
the unity of opinion.

John F. Kennedy

~

*Man matures through work
which inspires him to difficult good.*

Pope John Paul II

~

*The ascension of the soul is like a cord of
silk that enables devout intention, groping
in the darkness, to find the path to the light.*

Umberto Eco

~

*Feeling sorry for people is not enough.
Act to help them.*

Shramadana guideline

~

*Keep your mind free of divisions and
distinctions. When your mind is detached, simple,
quiet, then all things can exist in harmony, and you
begin to perceive the subtle truth.*

Lao Tzu

~

Mother Teresa to Diana:

"To heal other people you have to suffer yourself."

Diana's reply to Mother Teresa:

" Death doesn't frighten me."

*Inscription on the gates of Kensington Palace
in the days of mourning
before the funeral of
Diana, Princess of Wales:*

*"To live in the hearts of those
we leave behind is not to die."*

Thomas Campbell

~

Infinite sharing is the law of
God's inner life.

Thomas Merton

~

I didn't know I was a slave until I found out
I couldn't do the things I wanted.

Frederick Douglass

~

The charity that is a trifle to us
can be precious to others.

Homer

~

He who knows others is learned;
he who knows himself is wise.

Lao Tzu

~

Let the waters settle
you will see stars and moon
mirrored in your being.

Rumi
~

Infinite silence is the mind of God.
It is a mind that can create anything
out of the field of pure potentiality.
Infinite silence contains
Infinite dynamism.
Practice silence
and you will acquire
silent knowledge.
In this silent knowledge
is a computing system that is
far more precise
and far more accurate
and far more powerful
than anything that is contained
in the boundaries of rational thought.

Deepak Chopra
~

Hypocrisy is a fashionable vice,
and all fashionable vices
pass for virtues.

Moliere

~

Historians relate not so much
what is done as what they
would have believed.

Benjamin Franklin

~

Hell has three gates:
lust, anger, and greed.

Bhagavad Gita

~

Learn what you are and be such.

Pindar

~

All men should strive to learn before they
die what they are running from,
and to, and why.

James Thurber

~

To love oneself is the beginning
of a life-long romance.

Oscar Wilde

~

Religions are such stuff as dreams
are made of.

H.G. Wells

~

Religion is the reaction of human nature
to its search for God.

Alfred North Whitehead
~

We have just enough religion to make us
hate, but not enough to make us
love one another.

Jonathan Swift
~

Knowledge and history
are the enemies of religion.

Napoleon I
~

Matters of religion should never be matters
of controversy. We neither argue with a
lover about his taste, nor condemn him, if
we are just, for knowing
so human a passion.

George Santayana
~

American Wisdom

Congress
shall make no law respecting
an establishment of religion,
or prohibiting
the exercise thereof;
or abridging
the freedom of speech,
or of the press,
or the right of the people
peaceably to assemble,
and to petition
the Government for
a redress of grievances.

*Amendment I
to the Constitution of
The United States of America (1791)*

~

No person, demeaning himself in a peaceable and orderly manner, shall ever be molested on account of his mode of worship or religious sentiments, in the said territory.

Article I
The Northwest Ordinance (1787)

~

The inhabitants of the ceded territories shall be secured in the free exercise of their religion, without any restriction...

Article V
Adams-Onis Treaty:
U.S. Title to the Floridas (1819)

~

We have been preserved,

these many years, in peace and prosperity.
We have grown in numbers,
wealth and power,
as no other nation has ever grown.
But we have forgotten God.
We have forgotten the gracious hand which pre-
served us in peace,
and multiplied and enriched
and strengthened us;
and we have vainly imagined,
in the deceitfulness of our hearts,
that all these blessings were produced
by some superior wisdom and virtue of our own.
Intoxicated with unbroken success,
we have become too self-sufficient
to feel the necessity of redeeming and preserving
grace,
too proud to pray
to the God that made us!
It behooves us, then,
to humble ourselves before the offended Power,
to confess our national sins, and
to pray for
clemency and
forgiveness.

President Abraham Lincoln
Proclaiming A Day Of National Fasting,
March 30, 1863

This country
cannot afford
to be
materially rich
and spiritually poor.

President John F. Kennedy

~

Make yourself sheep
and the wolves
will eat you.

Benjamin Franklin

~

Religion
is for people
who want to avoid
the experience
of God.

Carl Jung

~

Question with boldness
even the existence of God;
because if there be one,
He must approve the homage of
Reason rather than that of
blindfolded Fear.

Thomas Jefferson

~

Religion has too often
become the debasing negative
energy that demands that we
praise religion and ignore man.

Gerry Spence

~

However sugarcoated and
ambiguous, every form of
authoritarianism must start with
a belief in some group's greater
right to power, whether that right
is justified by sex, race, class,
religion or all four.

Gloria Steinem

~

Surgeon General's Warning:

Smoking Causes
Lung Cancer,
Heart Disease,
Emphysema,
And May Complicate Pregnancy.

An American Cigarette Package

At _____
we take pride in
making a quality product.

Same American Cigarette Package

I believe
the doctor of the future
will be a teacher
as well as a physician.
His real job will be
to teach people how to be healthy.
Doctors will be even busier
than they are now
because it is a lot harder
to keep people well
than it is
just to get them
over a sickness.

Dr. D.C. Jarvis
Author of
"Folk Medicine: A New England
Almanac of Natural Health Care
From a Noted Vermont Country Doctor."

Is life so dear,
or peace so sweet,
as to be purchased
at the price of chains
and slavery?
Forbid it, Almighty God!
I know not what course
others may take;
but as for me,
give me liberty,
or give me
death!

Patrick Henry, 1775

When in the course
of human events,
it becomes necessary
for one people
to dissolve the political bands
which have connected them
with another,
and to assume among
the Powers of the earth,
the separate and equal station
to which the Laws of Nature
and of Nature's God entitle them,
a decent respect to the opinions
of mankind requires that they
should declare the causes which
impel them to the separation.

The first paragraph of
The Declaration of Independence, 1776

And for the support of this
Declaration,
with a firm reliance on
the Protection of
Divine Providence,
we mutually pledge
to each other
our Lives,
our Fortunes
and our Sacred Honor.

*The last sentence of
The Declaration of Independence, 1776*

When we let freedom ring,
when we let it ring from
every village and every hamlet,
from every state and every city,
we will be able to speed up that
day when all God's children,
black men and white men,
Jews and Gentiles, Protestants
and Catholics, will be able to join
hands and sing in the words
the old Negro spiritual
"Free at last! free at last!
thank God Almighty,
we are free at last!"

*Martin Luther King, Jr.,
from "I Have a Dream"*

Then conquer
we must,
when our cause
is just,
And this be our motto—
"In God is our Trust!"
And the
star-spangled banner
in triumph shall wave,
O'er the land
of the free
and the home
of the brave.

"The Star-Spangled Banner"
1814

The thing that impresses me
most about America
is the way parents
obey their children.

Duke of Windsor
"Look," March 5, 1957

~

If we ever pass out
as a great nation
we ought to put on our
tombstone "America died from
a delusion that she had moral
leadership."

Will Rogers,
"The Autobiography of Will Rogers"
1949

You know
what's wrong with America?
Americans.

You know what's right with
America?
Americans.

Marianne Williamson

~

American youth attributes much
more importance to arriving
at driver's license age than
at voting age.

Marshall McLuhan

~

You in the West have
the spiritually poorest of the poor
much more than you have
the physically poor.
Often among the rich
are very spiritually poor people.
I find it easy to give a plate of rice
to a hungry person,
to furnish a bed
to a person who has no bed,
but to console or to remove
the bitterness, anger,
and loneliness
that comes from being
spiritually deprived
that takes a long time.

Mother Teresa

We have opened a home
in New York for AIDS patients,
who find themselves among the
most unwanted people of today.
What a tremendous change
has been brought about in their
lives just because of a few sisters
who take care of them and
have made a home for them.
A place, perhaps the only place,
where they feel loved, where they
are somebody to someone. This
has changed their lives in such a
way that they die a most beautiful
death. Not one of them has yet
died in distress.

Mother Teresa

Nothing is more evident both in reason and The Holy Scriptures, than that religion is ever a matter between God and individuals; and therefore, no man or men can impose any religious test without invading the essential prerogatives of our Lord Jesus Christ... And let the history of all nations be searched and it will appear that the imposing of religious tests had been the greatest engine of tyranny in the world.

Baptist Minister Reverend Isaac Backus defending
Article 6 of the Constitution, 1787

~

To come to the true principle, the business of civil government is to protect the citizen and his rights. Civil government has no business to meddle with the private opinions of the people. I am accountable not to man, but to God, for the religious opinions which I embrace. A test law is the offspring of error and spirit of persecution. Legislatures have no right to set up an inquisition and examine into the private opinions of men.

Oliver Ellsworth, 12-17-1787, delegate to
Federal Constitutional Convention in Philadelphia,
member of US Congress, Chief Justice of US Supreme Court

Worldly
Wisdom
From A to Z

This is the sum of all true righteousnes:
Treat others, as thou wouldst thyself be treated.
Do nothing to thy neighbor,
Which hereafter thou wouldst not
have thy neighbor do to thee.

Hinduism

~

Hurt not others with that
which pains yourself.

Buddhism

~

Do unto all men as you would wish to
have done to you;
And reject for others what you
reject for yourselves.

Islam

~

Do unto others as you would have them do unto you,
for this is the law and the prophets.

Christianity

~

*Tzu-Kung asked: "Is there one principle upon
which one's whole life may proceed?"
The Master replied, "Is not Reciprocity
such a principle?—
What you do not yourself desire,
do not put before others."*

Confucianism

~

*What is harmful to yourself
do not to your fellow man.
That is the whole of the Torah.
The rest is commentary.*

Judaism

~

*There is but one God whose name is true.
He is the creator, immortal, unborn, self-existent.*

Sikhism

~

*There is one God and Father of all,
Who is above all, and through all,
And in you all.*

Christianity

~

*Remember even when alone that
the Divine is everywhere.*

Confucianism

~

*He is the one God hidden in all beings, all-pervading,
The Self within all beings, watching over all worlds,
dwelling in all beings, the witness, the perceiver.*

Hinduism

~

*Have we not all one Father?
Has not one God created us?*

Judaism

~

*Regard Heaven as your father, Earth as your mother,
and all things as your brothers and sisters.*

Shintoism

~

*A man obtains a proper rule of action
by looking on his neighbor as himself.*

Hinduism

~

Thou shalt love thy neighbor as thyself.

Judaism

~

Full of love for all things in the world,
practicing virtue in order to benefit others,
this man alone is happy.

Buddhism

~

A new commandment I give to you, That you love one
another; even as I have loved you...
by this all men will know that you are my disciples,
if you have love for one another.

Christianity

~

Seek to be in harmony with all your neighbors;
Live in amity with your brethren.

Confucianism

~

To speak ill of anyone is to speak ill of yourself.
—Afghanistan

The child hates the one who gives him all he wants.
—Africa

If you fear God you won't fear humans.
—Albania

A book is a little garden carried in the pocket.
—Arabia

*If a rich man dies, all the world is moved; if a poor
man dies, nobody knows it.*
—Armenia

The situation is hopeless, but not serious.
—Austria

Cunning is better than strength.
—Bahamas

The best mirror is an old friend.
—Balearic Isles

*A woman's clothes are the price
her husband pays for peace.*
—Bantu Proverb

Truth may walk through the world unarmed.
—Bedouin Proverbs

God heals, but the doctor gets paid.
—Belgium

If God were not forgiving, heaven would be empty.
—Berber Proverb

The eyes of all cheats are full of tears.
—Bosnia

Frugality is the sure guardian of our virtues.
—Brahman Proverb

He who knows nothing, doubts nothing.
—Brazil

If you cannot serve, you cannot rule
—Bulgaria

God gives, but he doesn't sell.
—Burundi

Cultivate a heart of love that knows no danger.
—Cambodia

Better a mistake at the beginning than the end.
—Cameroon

Do not put all your eggs in one basket.
—Canada

A person without a spouse is like a vase
without flowers.
—Catalonian Proverb

A man with too much ambition cannot sleep in peace.
—Chad

Anger is always more harmful than the insult
that caused it.
—China

The law is good, but people are not.
—China

One man tells a lie, dozens repeat it as the truth.
—China

One day of hunger is not starvation.
—Congo

*Much more than you have sown will
grow in your garden.*
—Croatia

Life is short but a smile takes barely a second.
—Cuba

*We must convince by reason, not prescribe
by tradition.*
—Cyprus

Not everybody is as bad as he is dressed.
—Denmark

A chain is as strong as its weakest link.
—Denmark

A beautiful thing is never perfect.
—Egypt

Silence is the best answer to the stupid.
—Egypt

Actions speak louder than words.
—England

Well begun is half done.
—England

Never pet a bear unless it is a rug.
—Eskimo Proverb

Move your neck according to the music.
—Ethiopia

The world is a good teacher, but it charges a huge fee.
—Finland

Loving with the eyes only has blinded a lot of fools.
—France

To be a fool at the right time is an art.
—France

Avoid the evil, and it will avoid thee.
—Gaelic Proverb

In America an hour is forty minutes.
—Germany

He who is quick to borrow, is slow to pay.
—Germany

For lazy people it is always party time.
—Greece

The grumbling mother-in-law forgets that
she once was a bride.
—Greece

If you want your eggs hatched, sit on them yourself.
—Haiti

No one is so poor as an ignorant person.
—Hebrew Proverb

To do nothing teaches evil.
—Holland

Need is not governed by the law.
—Iceland

Useless wisdom is double foolishness.
—India

We admire what we do not understand.
—India

A friend is a poem.
—Iran

A greedy man is always poor.
—Iran

Tell me who your friends are,
and I'll tell you who you are.
—Iraq

It takes time to build castles.
—Ireland

Do not try to make yourself so big,
you are not so small.
—Israel

Half a brain is enough for him who says little.
—Italy

A good conscience is better than a big wage.
—Jamaica

Abuse often starts with praise.
—Japan

Boasting begins where wisdom stops.
—Japan

If you receive a gift don't measure it.
—Kenya

Words have no wings but they
can fly a thousand miles.
—*Korea*

Happiness flies away from those who want it most.
—*Laos*

Freedom does not lengthen life.
—*Latvia*

A clear conscience shines not only in the eyes.
—*Lebanon*

Words are but dwarfs, examples are giants.
—*Luxembourg*

Sorrow is like a precious treasure,
shown only to friends.
—*Madagascar*

Anger has no eyes.
—*Malaysia*

The eleventh commandment:
Thou shalt not contradict.
—*Mexico*

Wealth is both an enemy and a friend.
—Nepal

Not to know is bad; not to want to know is worse.
—Nigeria

It is the law that judges, not the judge.
—Norway

When the mouth stumbles, it is worse than
when the foot does.
—Oji (West Africa)

The ignorant is his own enemy.
—Palestine

The hardest person to wake up is the person
who is already awake.
—Philippines

Nowadays you have to go heaven to meet an angel.
—Poland

When you talk about the sun, you will see her beams.
—Quebecois Proverb

Adversity makes a man wise, not rich.
—Romania

Abundance, like want, ruins many.
—Romania

If age and experience came at birth,
we would have neither youth nor mirth.
—Russia

Everyday is a messenger from God.
—Russia

Envy sees the sea but not the rocks.
—Russia

Stones decay; words last.
—Samoa

Sin is carried in the mouth.
—Samoa

There are none so deaf as those who
will not hear advice.
—Sanskrit Proverb

The eyes do not see what the mind does not want.
—Sanskrit Proverb

The hand that rocks the cradle rules the world.
—Scotland

Diet cures more than Doctors.
—Scotland

Money and the devil know no rest.
—Serbia

Unspoken words cannot be noted.
—Sicily

The less things change, the more they
remain the same.
—Sicily

You are not great just because you say you are.
—South Africa

The lazybones must work twice.
—South America

Advise no one to go to war or to marry.
—Spain

Of what you see, believe very little,
of what you are told, nothing.
—Spain

He who never has enough never has anything.
—Spain

Men are just as God made them –
and a little worse.
—Spain

Happiness does not give, it only lends.
—Sweden

A life without love is like a year without summer.
—Sweden

Being young is a fault which improves daily.
—Sweden

It is easier to criticize than to do better.
—Switzerland

The poor lack much, but the greedy more.
—Switzerland

It is cruelty to the innocent not to punish the guilty.
—Syria

Work is the source of all good.
—Thailand

There is no other happiness but peace.
—Thailand

Beat a Chinese long enough and he will talk Tibetan.
—Tibet

Goodness speaks in a whisper, evil shouts.
—Tibet

Any fool can say "Ah" – you need
intelligence to say "Yes."
—Tibet

Abundance doesn't know contentment,
but contentment knows abundance.
—Turkey

Everyone admires his own character.
—Turkey

A stupid friend is a greater plague than a wise enemy.
—Turkey

He who lives on hope, dies of starvation.
—Turkey

He who tells no lies will not grow up.
—Uganda

To see a friend no road is too long.
—Ukraine

Fools love not the wise, drunkards love not the sober.
—Ukraine

Bragging saves advertising.
—United States

Every cloud has a silver lining.
—United States

Honesty is like an icicle – once it melts,
that's the end of it.
—United States

Years know more than books.
—United States

Money talks – everything else walks.
—United States

There is nothing hidden between heaven and earth.
—Venezuela

Enter alcohol, exit words.
—Vietnam

Never forget benefits done you, regardless how small.
—Vietnam

Better to die than to live on with a bad reputation.
—Vietnam

Life is a temporary stop, death is the journey home.
—Vietnam

Willing is a good man, but Able is a better one.
—Virgin Islands

Anger is the mother of treachery.
—Wales

If every fool wore a crown, we should all be kings.
—Wales

Do good and then do it again.
—Wales

Better warn than be warned.
—Walloon Proverb

Whoever does not help himself cannot help others.
—Yemen

The master of the people is their servant.
—Yemen

You can wash your body but not your soul.
—Yiddish Proverb

"For example" is not proof.
—Yiddish Proverb

If it must always be better, it can never be good
enough.
—Yiddish Proverb

If your mouth were a knife it would cut off your lips.
—Zimbabwe

He who hates, hates himself.
—Zulu Proverb

Everyday
Wisdom

Everyday Wisdom

If God is indeed everywhere, then that would also mean that God is in each one of us. The Greater Intelligence is in each one of us. The potential for greatness is in each one of us. In fact, God is in the seemingly ordinary, everyday situations of your life.

Just think that the Master Mind is moving through you at any given moment! It is up to us, though, to be able to get in contact with the "god nature" in each one of us. In times of stress, we can listen to the wisdom of peace. In times of despair, we can hear the words of hope.

It is easy to "see God" in the majesty of the Rocky Mountains, or in the vast depths of the clear blue seas. But it seems to be more difficult to see the Formless One in, say, a bagel. Or in a traffic jam full of honking cars. Or in a child who is crying at the zoo. Or in your subordinates at the office who rely upon your guidance. The truth is that God is everywhere, in everything, and everyone has the potential to realize this!

We still think that God is some form of a man. We even call God "He" in some scriptures. No wonder some people have thoughts and opinions that God is endowed with human characteristics. Words cannot possibly come close to accurately or perfectly describing the Master of the Universe, the Almighty! We tend to project onto God our opinions of what we would want God to be. We think God is jealous and wrathful because we are jealous and wrathful. We have made a mess of trying to "pin God down" as if we could have the power to interview Him and ask Him some really tough questions that would cause Him to stumble. No – if there is a God, then most religions hold God to be infinitely more powerful, more intelligent, more sane, more moral, and certainly more perfect than us tiny human beings. Think about it.

It is up to us to see this great power and majesty in everything on earth despite our egos telling us that we are "better" than another, more religious than another, or more pious than another. It cannot be so. What God sees in us we need to see in others also. This "seeing" can be extended throughout the world, but we must get over our smaller beliefs that we are right and everyone else is wrong. Would you rather be right, or be at peace?

Look at it this way: human beings are limited as to the number of languages we are fluent in. Now do you think that God has limitations too? It would seem as if that is definitely not the case. Perhaps God has spoken to everyone in the language that was "right" for them.

Otherwise the Hebrew would not have understood Japanese, right?

Our arrogance rears its ugly head when we believe that our God is the only God there is. But He would have let everybody know that if it was true, right? So God told everybody about Him. He told everybody—in their native language – that He exists. That is a fact. Get over yourself. Just because you do not speak Chinese does not mean the content of the New Testament cannot be found in Taoism. Only the form is different. The truth is true no matter who says it, writes it, reads it, follows it. In this section try to see the everyday wisdom in each of the statements. God speaks through everything and everyone. Why? Because God knows not our limits to expression. God, in all His infiniteness, can express Himself anywhere, at any time, to anybody, and through anybody.

I cannot live without books.

Thomas Jefferson

~

Books are the best of things.

Ralph Waldo Emerson

~

*Most of today's books have an air of
having been written in one day
from books read the night before.*

Chamfort, Maximes et Pensees (1805)

~

*There is no such thing as a moral or
immoral book. Books are well written,
or badly written. That is all.*

Oscar Wilde

~

*Conversation enriches the understanding
but solitude is the school of genius;
and the uniformity of a work denotes
the hand of a single artist.*

Edward Gibbon

~

*No man ever will unfold the capacities
of his own intellect who does not at least
checker his life with solitude.*

De Quincey

~

*We must reserve a little back-shop,
all our own, entirely free, wherein to establish our
true liberty and principal retreat and solitude.*

Montaigne

~

The person who sows a single beautiful thought in the mind of another, renders the world a greater service than that rendered by all the faultfinders combined.

Napoleon Hill

~

And just as history will decide whether the leaders of today's world employed the atom to destroy the world or rebuild it mankind's benefit, so will history decide whether today's broadcasters employed their powerful voice to enrich people or debase them.

FCC Chairman, Newton N. Minow

~

Superior people understand justice, small people understand profit.

Confucius

~

The government itself, which is the only mode which the people have chosen to execute their will, is equally liable to be abused and perverted before the people can act through it.

Henry David Thoreau

~

People are pure when government is unobtrusive, people are wanting when government is invasive.

Lao Tzu

~

I am opposing a social order in which it is possible for one man who does absolutely nothing that is useful to amass a fortune of hundreds of millions of dollars, while millions of men and women who work all the days of their lives secure barely enough for a wretched existence.

Prisoner Eugene Victor Debs

~

The body is the spirit incognito.

Sandor McNab

~

The foolish do not look beyond physical
appearances to see my true nature
as the Lord of all creation.
The knowledge of such
deluded people is empty;
their lives are fraught with disaster and evil
and their work and hopes are all in vain.

Sri Krishna

~

Neglecting to broaden their view has kept some men
doing one thing all their lives.

Napoleon Hill

~

When we're afraid, everything rustles.

Sophocles

~

Every difficulty slurred over
will be a ghost to disturb your repose later on.

Chopin

~

If you've always done it that way,
it's probably wrong.

Charles Kettering

~

What we need is more people
who specialize in the impossible.

Theodore Roethke

~

Travel seems not just a way of having a good time,
but something that every self-respecting
citizen ought to undertake, like a high-fiber diet,
say, or, a deodorant.

Jan Morris

~

How does it feel to be without a home,
like a complete unknown,
like a rolling stone?

Bob Dylan

~

Do what you can, with what you have,
where you are.

Theodore Roosevelt

~

There is much more to this life than just increasing its speed.

Linda Greep

~

It's all one to me if a man comes from Sing Sing or Harvard. We hire a man, not his history.

Henry Ford

~

Men take only their needs into consideration, never their abilities.

Napoleon Bonaparte

~

I shall tell you a secret, my friend.
Do not wait for the last judgment,
it takes place every day.

Albert Camus

~

It used to be that people needed
products to survive. Now products need
people to survive.

Nicholas Johnson

~

The total absence of humor
from the bible
is one of the most singular things
in all literature.

Ashley Montagu

~

The sower may mistake and sow his peas crookedly; the peas make no mistake, but come up and show his line.

Emerson, Journals, 1843

~

Anger as soon as fed is dead –
'Tis starving makes it fat.

Emily Dickenson, Poem

~

The trouble with a kitten is
That
eventually it becomes a cat.

Ogden Nash, "The Kitten"

~

*Outside show is a poor substitute
for inner worth.*

Aesop

~

Architecture is inhabited sculpture

Constantin Brancusi

~

*In a philosophical dispute, he gains
most who is defeated,
since he learns most.*

Epicurus, "Vatican Sayings."

~

*The artist is the most interesting of all
phenomena, for he represents creativity,
the definition of man.*

*Allan Bloom,
"The Closing of the American Mind"*

~

*We must never forget that art is not a
form of propaganda;
it is a form of truth.*

John F. Kennedy

~

*I already have a wife,
who is too much for me;
one who keeps me struggling on.
It is my art, and my works
are my children.*

Michelangelo

~

*The hot blue flame
is the hottest part of the flame.*

Tim Pitzer

~

*The world has a birthday everyday
and everyday everyone needs to
remember to celebrate it.*

Randall Blaum

~

I don't approve of my attitude.

Katharine Hepburn

~

*I can do anything tomorrow
because it doesn't exist.*

Ernest Hemingway

~

Boredom: the desire for desires.

Leo Tolstoy

~

*What is good for the swarm
is not good for the bee.*

Marcus Aurelius

~

*When you stand in Truth,
nothing can hurt you.
No one can accuse you of anything
except that you went ahead
and told the darn ol' Truth... AGAIN!*

Sandi McFerran

~

The other day the "whozzits" fell onto the "whatchamacallit" and the whole thing went cattywampus!

Mabel Blaum

~

The car has become an article of dress without which we feel uncertain, unclad, and incomplete.

Marshall McLuhan

~

Adam and Eve had many advantages, but the principal one was that they escaped teething.

Mark Twain

~

Things are beautiful if you love them.

Jean Anouilh

~

*We believe what we want to believe ,
what we like to believe, what suits our
prejudices and fuels our passions.*

Sydney J. Harris

~

*If you're going to age successfully, you have to
devote time to keeping your body and your
brain in good working order.*

*Stan Hinden, retired Washington Post financial
writer and columnist for "Retirement Journal."*

~

*It's only when we truly know and understand that we
have a limited time on earth – and that we have no
way of knowing when our time is up – that we will
begin to live each day to the fullest, as if it were the
only one we had.*

Elisabeth Kübler-Ross

~

*When you live in the moment, you don't put off
enjoying your life.*

Oprah

~

*Pretty soon, your baby could be
wearing someone else's genes.*

*Advertisement for "Health"
on the Discovery Channel*

~

*Draco Dormiens Nunquam Titillandus
(Never tickle a sleeping dragon)*

Motto for Harry Potter's boarding school

~

This is the true story of seven strangers, picked to live in a house, and have their lives taped, to find out what happens when people stop being polite and start getting real. To be successful, you'll have to learn that you can rise to any challenge. If you fail, you'll discover the true meaning of teamwork.

MTV's Real World

~

We have spent nearly £55-million putting computers in virtually every classroom – many in less well-off areas. And we're now rolling out Internet cafes in our stores to provide access to our customers. We need to ensure a competitive world for Internet services. We want an open and easy-to-use system of access to the home; safe but unfettered by cumbersome bureaucracy.

Terry Leahy, Chief Executive, Tesco, The World's Leading Online Grocery Store and More! (www.tesco.com)

~

Wisdom
for
Business

IS IT ONLY ABOUT MONEY?

NO!

Money is such a small perception of who you really are. And if you think that your self-worth is defined by how much money you make, then not only do you not understand money, but you do not understand yourself. You do not understand the value of yourself, and you do not understand the value of money.

READ ON GENTLE ONES...

What is our business in life?

It has been said that the real reason we are all here is to serve. Okay... but serve "what" and to "whom?" If we are to express the divine glory of the gods, or God, then our existence must transcend the normal, everyday goals of life. We are supposed to be living with the highest and best of the human values: love, kindness, truth, goodness, abundance, gentleness and joy. The fulfillment of these virtues is also fulfilling our Divine mission to serve one another. While we cannot change the world, we can change our inner world to the point that our perception of the outer world changes significantly. Change your mind and change your life! All of us have, at some point, forgotten who we really are and why we came here. None of us were meant to grovel in poverty, none of us were meant to withhold the truth from another, none of us were meant to keep someone from shining at their brightest. Our Ultimate business in this life is to become aware of the glory that is all around us and in everyone.

This is the business of LIVING!

Common Questions About Business

1. What is work?
2. What is business?
3. What is my real career?
4. What is real leadership?
5. What is the information age really about?

Common Myths About Business

1. Work is slavery…only 20 years left.

2. Business is all about making money for big, evil, greedy corporations like mine!!

3. My real career is what I have to do, not what I really want to do.

4. Real leadership is only for bosses because "That's why they get paid the big bucks."

5. The information age is really a conspiracy theory forcing me to constantly spend money upgrading all my software until I neglect my job, my family, and myself so much that I do nothing but try to decipher poorly translated, HUGE computer manuals that are as big as the computer itself.

What is work? and what is not work?
are the questions that perplex the wisest of men.

Bhagavad Gita

~

In the sweat of thy face shalt thou eat bread,
till thou return unto the ground;
for out of it wast thou taken.

Genesis 3:16

~

He that can work
is born a king of something.

Thomas Carlyle

~

Toil, says the proverb, is the sire of fame.

Euripides

~

Men for the sake of getting a living forget to live.

Margaret Fuller

~

Human happiness is the true odor of growth,
the sweet exhalation of work.

David Grayson

~

Serious occupation is labor that has reference
to some want.

Hegel

~

When work is a pleasure, life is a joy!
When work is a duty, life is slavery.

Maxim Gorky

~

The Seven Laws of Money

1. Do what you love, money will follow.

2. You must follow money's rules about supply, demand, budgets, saving, borrowing.

3. "Money" is not what you want; you want what money can buy.

4. To the extent that you desire money it will enslave you and you will be obsessed by it. (Had you noticed?)

5. You cannot GIVE money without GETTING money back in some form. The law of reciprocity says that having and giving are the same thing.

6. The "flow" of money is never supposed to stop. If you do stop it, like receiving money as a gift without some form of "thank you" or giving back, then you will be haunted by feelings of desire for more.

7. There is a state of being and living in this world that requires ZERO MONEY in order to live: dreams, meditation, peace.

The 11 Characteristics of Success

1. **Be Industrious:** We must work in order to survive that's true. But if we must work, we must do it *well* by being industrious. Even the body was designed for work, otherwise it withers away and dies quickly from neglect.

2. **Be Intelligent:** No one gets by in this world by flaking out – eventually everything you ignored or missed or didn't spend time on will come back to haunt you. Listen, watch, and ACT! Don't get "skilled," get educated.

3. **Be Ethical:** You should always have an "ethical force-field" around you and not the "vacuum of darkness" that surrounds unethical people.

4. **Be Enthusiastic:** If you bore yourself, you might bore someone else too! Get happy! You are responsible for your own feelings, nobody else is. Get over yourself.

5. **Be Involved:** this is your life, not your neighbor's! If not YOU, then WHO? If you do not follow your heart in your work, then you are "ignoring" God's gifts in yourself.

6. **Have Interpersonal relationships:** be nice to others and they will be nice to you. You have to love others before you understand them. Friends: there's nothing like 'em.

7. **Be Creative and open minded:** Two words: Michelangelo and Edison. If they had said "No," we would not have any ART or LIGHT BULBS with which to see the art!

8. **Be Critical:** be able to give it *constructively* and not *destructively*. Critical people are not thin-skinned. The more respected your criticism, the more respected you will be.

9. **Be Positive:** A little advice on this one: happy people are attracted to *happy people*. Get it? Positive energy is literally an attractive force while being negative and playing small are repelling forces of energy. When you are happy, living your life with joy, then all will come to you. When you are negative, nothing comes to you. YOU have to change, and the world will appear to change with you.

10. **Have a sense of humor:** Happiness and laughter are the best medicines in the world. A life without laughter is like a body without soul.

11. **And Finally!!!** The eleventh characteristic is the "glue" that holds it all together. Ready? Successful people don't care about "success." It is only the icing on the cake but you need the cake *first* or else the icing won't stick. "Non-attachment."

You can't change what you don't acknowledge.

Philip C. McGraw, Ph.D.

~

"Protocol" is the way we are to carry ourselves in business and in life. Here is what India has to say about "Protocol:"

The eye of knowledge sees with the most clarity.
Truth is the greatest atonement.
Attachment is the worst of all sorrows.
Detachment is the source of lasting happiness.

The Vedas

~

People of wisdom and character are devoted to action. People without strength and conviction depend upon destiny. Prosperity forsakes those who rely on destiny and favors those who act.

The Vedas

~

Because the Customer

Because the customer has a **need**, we have a job to do.

~

Because the customer has a choice, we must be
the **better choice.**

~

Because the customer has sensibilities, we must be
considerate.

~

Because the customer has an urgency, we must be
quick.

~

Because the customer is unique, we must be
flexible.

~

Because the customer has high expectations, we must
excel.

~

Because the customer has **influence,** we have hope of
more customers.

~

Because of the customer, **we exist.**

~

Creed for San Francisco's famous Sears Restaurant
near Union Square.

It is weariness to keep toiling at the same things
so that one becomes ruled by them.

Heraclitus

~

The door of success is labeled
ENTRANCE and EXIT.

Yiddish saying

~

The Talmud says: Who is really rich?

Rabbi Yose used to say:
One who has a bathroom
near his dining room.

Rabbi Meir used to say:
One who derives inner peace
from his fortune.

Shabbat 25 b

~

*Sages go first by putting themselves last,
survive by disregarding themselves.
It is by their selflessness that they manage
to fulfill themselves.*

Lao Tzu

~

Luck is preparation meeting opportunity.

Oprah Winfrey

~

*When you live your life with integrity, honesty
and gratefulness, you no longer
have to worry about how you
will make a living…
you ARE living.*

Marianne Williamson

~

*Work by its very nature (is) about violence –
to the spirit as well as to the body…. It is, above all
(or beneath all), about daily humiliations. To survive
the day is triumph enough for the walking
wounded…. It is about a search, too, for daily meaning as well as daily bread, for recognition as well as
cash, for astonishment rather than torpor; in short for
a sort of life rather than a Monday through Friday
dying. Perhaps immortality, too, is part of the quest –
to be remembered….*

Studs Terkel in "Working."

~

*If you don't back it up with performance and hard
work, talking doesn't mean a thing.*

Michael Jordan

~

*I believe that if God finds a person more useless than
me, He will do even greater things through her
because this work is His.*

Mother Teresa

We have the power
to let the current pass
through us,
use us,
produce the light
of the world.
Or we can refuse
to be used and allow
darkness to spread.

Mother Teresa

Those who believe
and whose hearts
find satisfaction
in the remembrance of God:
for without doubt,
in the remembrance of God
do hearts find satisfaction.
For those who believe and work righteousness,
is blessedness, and beautiful place of return.

Islam, Qur'an 13.28-19

~

I created human beings because I desired
to see you live a joyous life.

Tenrikyo, Ofudesaki 14.25

~

Thou dost show me the path of life;
in thy presence there is fullness of joy,
in thy right hand are pleasures for evermore.

Judaism and Christianity, Psalm 16.11

~

The Infinite is the source of joy.
There is no joy in the finite.
Only in the Infinite is there joy.
Ask to know the Infinite.

Hinduism, Chandogya Upanisad 7.23

~

Life is art.
The whole life of man is Self-expression.
The individual is an expression of God.
We suffer if we do not express ourselves.

Perfect Liberty Kyodan, Precepts 1-4

~

The Holy Spirit rests on him only
who has a joyous heart.

Judaism, Jerusalem Talmud, Sukkat 5.1

~

To seek gladness through righteous persistence
is the way to accord with heaven
and to respond to men.

Confucianism, I Ching 58: Joy.

~

*Happiness is spiritual, born of Truth and Love.
It is unselfish; therefore it cannot exist alone,
but requires all mankind to share it.*

Christian Science, Science and Health, 57

~

*Let us live happily, without hate amongst
those who hate. Let us dwell unhating
amidst hateful men.*

*Let us live happily, in good health amongst
those who are sick. Let us dwell in
good health amidst ailing men.*

*Let us live happily, without yearning for
sensual pleasures amongst those who
yearn for them. Let us dwell without
yearning amidst those who yearn.*

*Let us live happily, we have no impediments.
We shall subsist on joy even as the radiant gods.*

Buddhism, Dhammapada 197-200

~

How then to become true to the Creator?
How then to demolish the wall of illusion?
Through Obedience to His Ordinance and Will.

Sikhism, Adi Granth, Japuji 1, M.1, p.1

~

Son of Man! Veiled in My immemorial being and in
the ancient eternity of My essence,
I knew My love for thee;
therefore I created thee, have engraved on thee Mine
image, and revealed to thee My beauty.

Baha'i Faith Hidden Words of Baha'u'llah, Arabic 3

~

Do not try to develop what is natural to man;
develop what is natural to Heaven. He who develops
Heaven benefits life; he who develops man injures life.

Taoism, Chuang Tzu 19

~

Lord of all, hail unto thee!
The Soul of all, causing all acts,
Enjoying all, all life art thou!
Lord of all pleasure and delight!

Hinduism, Maitri Upanisad 5.1

~

*God's purpose in creating the universe was
to feel happiness when He saw the purpose of
goodness fulfilled in the Heavenly Kingdom, which
the whole creation, including man,
could have established... The purpose of
the universe's existence centered on man is
to return joy to God, the Creator.*

Unification Church, Divine Principle I.1.3.1

~

*Father, O mighty Force,
That Force which is in everything,
Come down between us, fill us,
Until we become like thee,
Until we become like thee.*

*African Traditional Religions,
Susu Prayer (Guinea)*

~

Conform yourselves to the character of God.

Islam, Hadith of Abu Nuaym

~

*Every spirit of man was innocent in the beginning; and
God having redeemed man from the fall, man became
again, in their infant state, innocent before God.*

Church of Jesus Christ of Latter-day Saints,
Doctrine of Covenants 93.38

~

*Religion is basically virtue, which is grounded
ultimately in the spiritual nature of man.*

Jainism, Kundakunda, Pravacanasara 7

~

*You may not see yourself growing up, but you
definitely know when you are sinning.*

*African Traditional Religions,
Akan Proverb (Ghana)*

~

Gentleness and goodness are the roots of humanity.

Confucianism, Book of Ritual 38.18

~

*You, therefore, must be perfect, as your heavenly
Father is perfect.*

Christianity, Matthew 5.48

~

One should be known as true
who in his heart bears truth –
His impurity of falsehood cast off,
his person should be washed clean.
One should be known as true
who to truth is devoted in love.

Sikhism, Adi Granth, Asa-ki-Var, M1,p.468

~

Rabbi Levitas of Yavneh said:

Be exceedingly humble,
for the hope of mankind
is the worm.

Pirke Avot, IV:4

~

Assertive and enterprising actions carried out by
those who are careless, inconsistent,
or unfortunate do not succeed.

The Vedas

~

A novice asked the Buddha, "What is goodness and what is greatness?" The Buddha replied, "To follow the Way and hold to what is true is good. When the will is in conformity with the Way, that is greatness."

Buddhism, Sutra of Forty-two sections 15

~

The whole world is sustained by God's charity; and the righteous are sustained by their own force.

Judaism, Talmud, Berakot 17b

~

*Undivided I am,
undivided my soul,
undivided my sight,
undivided my hearing,
undivided my in-breathing,
undivided my outbreathing,
undivided my diffusive breath;
undivided the whole of me.*

Hinduism, Atharva Veda 19.51.1

~

Blessed are the poor in spirit,
for theirs is the kingdom of heaven.
Blessed are those who mourn,
for they shall be comforted.
Blessed are those who are meek,
for they shall inherit the earth.
Blessed are those who hunger and thirst
for righteousness, for they shall be satisfied.
Blessed are the merciful, for they shall obtain mercy.
Blessed are the pure in heart, for they shall see God.
Blessed are the peacemakers,
for they shall be called sons of God.
Blessed are those who are persecuted
for righteousness' sake,
for theirs is the kingdom of heaven.

Christianity, Matthew 5.3-10: The Beatitudes

~

This holy instant would I give to You.
Be You in charge. For I would follow You,
Certain that Your direction gives me peace.

A Course in Miracles
Lessons 361 to 365

~

Intolerance just doesn't fly.

United Airlines

~

Strength in diversity. As a company that fosters diversity within itself, Bell Atlantic is proud to support Gay Pride 2000. Our lesbian and gay employees make a valuable contribution and reflect one of the many communities we serve. When every group has the chance to contribute we're all enriched.

Bell Atlantic

~

It's more than knowing who you are.
It's being who you are.
Freedom of expression. Do you have something you'd like to express?
Go ahead, come out with it.

Stolichnaya

~

Nourishing the community.

Odwalla

~

Reaching out to those in need is important, especially to those in our community who are living and coping with HIV. As a company involved in the discovery and development of new treatments for HIV, we understand that meeting the needs of people living with HIV includes patient support as well as medical therapy. We want to join with other companies, caregivers and the community in… Reaching out. Looking ahead.

DuPont Pharmaceuticals

~

Think globally. Spoon locally. Body. Bean. Soul. Body-healthy, earth-healthy goodness.

Silk soy milk

~

Ford Environmental Steward Luis Lara wants people to see the rain forest, but more than that, he wants a rain forest left for people to see.

Ford Motor Company

~

We help people trade practically anything on Earth.

Ebay

~

Our founding commitment is to customer satisfaction and the delivery of an educational and inspiring shopping experience.

Amazon.com

~

Our aspirations? Whatever our people can achieve.

Netdecisions.com

~

Peace of mind. Everyday.

Toyota

~

Run with the little guy…create some change.

Jones Soda company

~

We aim to create products that make intelligent use of the planet's resources; we support the rights of indigenous peoples; we do not conduct animal testing. In our view, these policies make good sense financially, environmentally, and morally. In fact, we believe they are the only sustainable path to the future.

Aveda Mission Statement

~

Opportunities for the universalization are plenty. The idea is not to wait but to lead in the process of universalizing. It's time to reexamine the existing market segmentation practices.

David Choi, Ph.D., principal of Diamond Technology

~

When you're green, you're growing.
When you're ripe, you rot.

Lisa Jansen

~

Victory is much more meaningful when it comes not just from the efforts of one person, but from the joint achievements of many. The euphoria is lasting when all participants lead with their hearts, winning not just for themselves but for one another.
Success is sweetest when it's shared.

Howard Schultz, Chairman and CEO of Starbucks Coffee Company

~

*I revolted in spirit
against the customs of society
and the laws of the state
that crushed my aspirations
and debarred me
from the pursuit
of every object
worthy of an
intelligent
rational
mind.*

Elizabeth Cady Stanton

~

*The companies, from Fortune 500s to mom and pops
to start-up entrepreneurs, that do the best job of
marketing to women will dominate every significant
product and service category.*

*Faith Popcorn, best-selling author of
The Popcorn Report
Clicking, and EVEolution*

~

Wisdom
for
Family

Wisdom for Family

WHAT DOES IT MEAN TO SAY that the family unit is vital and important to the survival of peace and harmony in the world? First of all, what is "family?" Then what is "important" and "survival?" Finally, what is "peace?" Have you ever looked at it this way— questioning *exactly* what is meant by these terms? The words used here are just that: words. They are the same words used in daily life, church sermons, theology, philosophy, science, and government work all over the planet. Keep in mind that we live on a planet and not some abstract idea of some kind of "kingdom" or "nation" or "political system" or "religion." Those are all abstract terms we use to label the world around us. They are mere labels and words. They do not accurately define the reality of the actual things themselves. The "word" is not the "thing."

In order to see another person clearly, without the lens of fear, we need to be able to see the other person as he is. We need to see the other person without our projections of fear, without the overbearing label of "sinner." How do you know what the other person has done in his life? Have you spent every minute with him? Do you live with him? For all you know, the very person you dislike might be an enlightened master! You just don't know. What if Jesus came down and tried to get to know you, but you said, "Look, man, I don't even *know you*." Exactly! If you don't know someone, how can you accurately assess him, judge him, or criticize him?

What happened to walking a mile in the other person's shoes before you even *think* of criticizing him? Love is always coming right at us, in a thousand different forms. The form of love may change, but the content of it stays the same. That is why we tend to see fear coming at us instead of love. We are conditioned to fear the world, even "to fear the Lord." Why? Fear causes us to live in increased fear of the other person. It is no wonder we end up seeing other people as our "crucifier" rather than our "savior." Our perception is up to us. Perception is not absolute. Contrary to popular *opinion,* perception is **not** reality. It only seems like it. Perceptions are false.

Perception gives us the *feeling* that the other person is different when really they are made up of the same kinds of atoms, chemicals, and elements of a typical carbon-based life form. Perception gives us the *feeling* that this world is real: we SEE with out eyes, we HEAR with our ears, we TASTE with our tongues, and yet each of us interprets these "senses" in a different way. Perception is not absolute, it varies from person to person.

Religion also *seems* to vary from person to person. That is why we need to get beyond our misperception that just because the *form* of the other's religion is different than our own, it does not mean that person is not on a path to the *same God.* God is the *content* and religion is the *form* that the content takes. Religion is the vehicle. If you interfere with someone's path, you may be attacking God's plan for salvation for that person. How do YOU know what God has planned for each and every person on the planet? Did God tell you everything over breakfast? Probably not.

Perhaps it is time for us to start following Star Trek's idea of The Prime Directive which stands for non-interference in someone else's way of life. Your interference will probably be interpreted as an attack, anyway. Think of yourself here: how would like it if someone always told you that everything you did was not *quite* right, that you just weren't good enough *yet,* that you will never be good enough, and that your life will always be under a veil of darkness known as... .sin? What is the point of self-induced tortuous thinking? What is the point of living in fear? What is the point of handing down stories generation after generation about fearing life – that anybody who looks different or thinks differently must be feared? This kind of mindset about the world is downright masochistic! It is this mindset that has perpetuated fear, violence, and destruction for centuries. It needs to stop.

The mindset of fear is anarchy compared to the mindset of living in peace. The fear mindset is a "get" mentality. It deals with finite resources, greediness, loss, and fear of not having enough. It openly invites unhealthy competition that leads to violence.

We need to replace the mindset of fear with the mindset of love, of peace, of giving—whatever you want to call it. The *form* that love may take might be different from the form you think love ought to take.

But once again, that would be your imposition on love, your dictate on what love should be – which is not love. This is why we need to concentrate on the *content* of love, rather than the form. Infinite love knows no limits. Only fear has limits because fear is afraid of the unknown, which is *limitless*. Fearful thoughts impose limits so it can always maintain a sense of control. In fact, if you are living fully in the present, you begin to find out that we are *not in control at all*. Only the force of life is in control. The universe "controls" us and not the other way around. We must learn to relax into reality, allowing it to show us what reality means instead of us forever imposing our will on everything in hopes to control, micromanage, perfect an already perfect universe created by God.

The power in the nature of the universe is limitless! It encompasses everything. It can even be called "God" if you want, remembering that God has no particular *form* of power, no particular *form* of love, no particular *form* of peace. God deals with content while our fearful mind insists on thinking in terms of fear, which is only artificial anyway. It has nothing to do with what is actually going on since it is only our *perception* of what is going on.

Fear is an illusion. Love is the only thing that is real. How can anyone be afraid of love? Well, over the centuries we have been taught and conditioned to fear our world, to fear our neighbor, to fear our own sexuality, to fear our own bodily functions, to fear our emotions, to fear our desires, even to fear "fear" itself. In short, we are conditioned to fear everything that makes us human. As human beings we are perfect but we are "perfect" in terms of an ideal. That kind of perfection is still just an idea – it is an abstract thought that has nothing whatsoever to do with actually being *human*. Put simply, you are a human *being* perfect, not a human *doing* perfect deeds. In other words, we are *already created perfect*. We just tend to get lost.

We are human beings first. We are citizens, and all those other labels, second. But first and foremost we are human beings. Can we start with that fact and move from there? Can we begin by loving each other a little bit more? Can we start by respecting each other a little bit more? Can we start shedding the skins of fear and begin basking in the glow of love and light at last? Which view of the world would you rather have: 1) that you are absolutely right and everyone else is wrong (isn't it tough to be alone?) – that your *form* of love is the one and only way to love and be loved in the world (which is the same as saying: my *religion* is the one and only way, my *job* is the one and only way, my *philosophy of life* is the one and only way, my *financial plan* is the one and only way...) or 2) that you know the fact that the form of love may change but your happiness is derived from the content of love. In other words: would you rather be happy than right?

We have been conditioned to "be happy" knowing that we are right. We believe we are happy when we follow the rules arbitrarily set by mankind. We believe we are happy when we make enough money, wear the right clothes, drive the right car, have a good hair day, smell right, look right, eat right, even *believe* in the "right" religion.

See how the fearful part of the mind thinks in terms of form? If you are thinking in terms of form, then you are thinking in terms of your preferences. Preferences change, they are not eternal, they are not absolute. Only love is absolute, never changing, always giving and receiving, always eternal, and ever expanding. Fear is finite, working in a static system, a closed system with limits. Love is the boundless universe full of God's stars!

The Holy Spirit is not saying: "What am I gonna *get* from you?" It says, "How may I help you? How may I serve you?" Love is gentle, yet strong. Love is focused, yet it flows like a river. Fear is limited while love is infinite. Since love is infinite, a heart full of love has the capacity to love everyone equally. What a relief! While the form of love may change in terms of the love a mother has for a child versus the same love she has for her husband, *the content does not change.* That is because love is just love and nothing else. Only love is real. Everything else is fear.

That brings us to where we are today. We live in a world in which "form" is different from person to person. Each person is unique, each person has a different form. All of us express love differently; however, all of us want and need to be loved.

So, you cannot hate the Republicans and love the Democrats, you cannot hate the Russians and love the British, you cannot love the African Americans and hate the White Anglo Saxon Protestants, you cannot hate the gays and lesbians and love the clergy, you cannot love your own child and hate the neighbor's children. That is not love, but fear. We always fear what we do not like or understand. Love is one and Absolute, it can be separated.

Although we may never consciously intend to hurt someone, what we need to do is *consciously intend to love someone.* Anyone! I don't care who it is! Love is needed today, not more violence, not more wars, not more "I know and you don't." That isn't love. That is arrogance and it smacks of small-minded thinking of a limited world.

God is infinite, love is infinite. We are created in God's image, therefore we have inherent within us an infinite capacity for love. We make mistakes, but that does not make us *mistaken.* We have fears, but that does not make us fearful. We may "be in love" with someone, but that is still not the same as loving things and people exactly as they are. We try to impose our will on what we want love to look like, and that is still the realm of fear that thinks only about *form.*

You have it within you to get beyond the illusions of fear. You have it within yourself to break down all the barriers that keep love out. God gave you "free will" to choose love rather than to choose a path of fear. God wants you to choose again, again, and again until you get it right.

You will get there eventually whether you believe it or not, whether you like it or not. Only the time you take to get there is up to you, but you cannot refuse what is your *true nature,* what is your *due inheritance,* which is love. Sooner or later the illusions of fear must break down. That is how the universe works. Everything is set up to make sure that you win. It is also set up to make sure that everybody else wins also. It is our mission to be like God, which means that we are expected to love, *everybody equally.* Who is this "everybody?" It is our *human* family. This section is about the one and only family each one of us have: *each other.*

The human family is one.

Love is one. There are not different kinds, no degrees, no separate parts or forms. Love is unchanged throughout, being Absolute, and the gift of God to His creation. Love does not judge. It cannot love at times and hate at others and still be called love, nor can it be given to one yet be withheld from another. To call this love is not to know it. To know love one must not attempt to choose between the righteous and the sinner and thus believe splitting God's creation into separate parts is somehow possible. Yet this is mankind's great delusion, forever keeping love at bay and darkness alive. The light of love is one, judging nothing since all is like itself, its energy as one, never to be destroyed. Nothing real can be threatened by what is false. Choose not to find salvation in separation by seeking your reality in false projections. Only love is real and nothing else exists. Love is the certain way out of all fear, forever extending its wisdom of perfect peace. Surely this is what you truly want.

That since wars begin
in the minds of men,
it is in the minds of men
that the defenses of peace
must be constructed;

That ignorance of each other's ways
and lives has been a common cause,
throughout the history of mankind,
of that suspicion and mistrust
between the peoples of the world
through which their differences have
all too often broken into war;

...that the peace must therefore
be founded, if it is not to fail, upon
the intellectual and moral solidarity
of mankind.

Excerpts from the Preamble to the United Nation's Charter for the United Nations Educational, Scientific and Cultural Organization (UNESCO)

Young people shall be brought up in the spirit of peace, justice, freedom, mutual respect and understanding in order to promote equal rights for all human beings and all nations, economic and social progress, disarmament and the maintenance of international peace and security.

Principle I of the Declaration on the Promotion among Youth of the Ideals of Peace, Mutual Respect and Understanding between Peoples by UNESCO, December 7, 1965

Young people shall be brought up in the knowledge of the dignity and equality of all men, without distinction as to race, color, ethnic origins or beliefs, and in respect for fundamental human rights and for the right of peoples to self-determination.

Principle III of the Declaration on the Promotion among Youth of the Ideals of Peace, Mutual Respect and Understanding between Peoples by UNESCO, December 7, 1965

A major aim in educating the young
shall be to develop all their faculties
and to train them to acquire higher
moral qualities, to be deeply attached
to noble ideals of peace, liberty,
the dignity and equality of all men,
and imbued with respect and
love for humanity and its
creative achievements.
To this end the family has an
important role to play.

Young people must become
conscious of their responsibilities
in the world they will be called upon
to manage and should be inspired
with confidence in a future of
happiness for mankind.

Principle VI of the Declaration on the Promotion among Youth
of the Ideals of Peace, Mutual Respect and Understanding

Recognizing my share of responsibility for the future of humanity especially for today's children and those of future generations, I pledge – in my daily life, in my family, my work, my community, my country and my region – to:

RESPECT THE LIFE
and dignity of every person without discrimination or prejudice;

PRACTICE ACTIVE NON-VIOLENCE,
rejecting violence in all its forms: physical, sexual, psychological, economical and social, in particular towards the most deprived and vulnerable such as children and adolescents;

SHARE MY TIME AND MATERIAL RESOURCES
in a spirit of generosity to put an end to exclusion, injustice and political and economic oppression;

DEFEND FREEDOM OF EXPRESSION AND CULTURAL DIVERSITY

giving preference always to dialogue
and listening rather than fanaticism,
defamation and the rejection of others;

PROMOTE CONSUMER BEHAVIOR THAT IS RESPONSIBLE

and development practices that respect
all forms of life and preserve the balance
of nature on the planet;

CONTRIBUTE TO THE DEVELOPMENT OF MY COMMUNITY,

with the full participation of women and
respect for democratic principles, in order
to create together new forms of solidarity.

*MANIFESTO 2000
FOR A CULTURE OF PEACE
AND NON-VIOLENCE*
The United Nations General Assembly UNESCO

Drafted by these Nobel Peace Prize Laureates:

Norman Borlaug, Adolfo Perez Esquivel, Dalai Lama, Mikhail
Sergeyevich Gorbachev, Maired Maguire, Nelson Mandela,
Rigoberta Menchu Tum, Shimon Peres, Jose Ramos Horta,
Joseph Roblat, Desmond Mpilo Tutu, David Trimble, Elie
Wiesel, Carlos Felipo, Ximenes Belo

While the world may be changing dramatically, remember that families are the backbone of our society. Families must endure forever.

Dave Wooley

~

May in this family discipline overcome indiscipline, peace discord, charity miserliness, devotion arrogance, the truth-spoken word the false-spoken word which destroys the holy order.

Zoroastrianism, Avesta, Yasna 60.5

~

Children are the clothes of a man.

African Traditional Religions
Yoruba Proverb (Nigeria)

~

Train up a child in the way he should go,
and when he is old he will not depart from it.

Judaism and Christianity, Proverbs 22.6

~

As the child, according to its natural
disposition, commits thousands of faults,
The father instructs and slights,
but again hugs him to his bosom.

Sikhism, Adi Granth, Sorath, M.5

~

Attend strictly to the commands of your
parents and the instructions of your teachers.
Serve your leader with diligence;
be upright of heart; eschew falsehood;
and be diligent in study; that you may conform
to the wishes of the heavenly spirit.

Shinto, Oracle of Temmangu

~

When women are honored, there the gods
are pleased; but where they are not honored,
no sacred rite yields rewards.
When the female relations live in grief,
the family soon wholly perished;
but that family where they are not unhappy
ever prospers.

Hinduism, Laws of Manu 3.56-57

~

He who loves his wife as himself; who honors
her more than himself; who rears his children
in the right path, and who marries them off
at the proper time of their life, concerning him
it is written: "And you will know
that your home is at peace."

Judaism, Talmud, Yebamot 62

~

When brothers agree, no fortress is so strong
as their common life.

Antisthenes (5ᵗʰ-4ᵗʰ Century, B.C.)

~

*The only rock I know that
stays steady, the only institution
I know that works,
is the family.*

Lee Iacocca

~

*Understanding and love require a wisdom
that comes only with age.*

Rollo May

~

*Peace is not made with friends.
Peace is made with enemies.*

Yitzhak Rabin

~

*Fair peace is becoming to men;
fierce anger belongs to beasts.*

Ovid (8 A.D.)

~

*Thus doth Ethiopia stretch forth her
hand from slavery,
to freedom and equality.*

Prince Hall, 1797

~

*An error means a child needs help,
not a reprimand or ridicule for doing
something wrong.*

Marva Collins

~

*Loving is letting go. Letting go of the need
to judge and the need to control.*

Susan L. Taylor, Editor in Chief, Essence Magazine

~

We are a nation with no geographic boundaries,
bound together through our beliefs.
We are like-minded individuals,
sharing a common vision,
pushing toward a world rid of color lines.

Janet Jackson, Rhythm Nation 1814

~

Do not merely listen to the word, and so deceive
yourselves. Do what it says. Anyone who listens to the
word but does not do what it says is like a man who
looks at his face in the mirror and, after looking at
himself, goes away and immediately forgets what he
looks like.

James 1:22-24

~

Judgment without mercy will be shown to anyone
who has not been merciful.
Mercy triumphs over judgment!

James 2:13

~

Wisdom
for
Yourself

Wisdom for Yourself

ONE COULD ARGUE that you have made no progress at all in your search for the Ultimate Truth. But that would only be an idea. It does not necessarily follow that you do **not** know the truth any more than the idea that you **do** know the truth just because you say that you know it. Either way we look at it, we use thought, memory, ideas, and words. They all mean nothing except they are all at the thought level rather than the level of experience. You can say you have experienced truth, and that may be a fact. But even the act of saying it, or describing it, is not the same as the actual truth. You are merely engaging you thought or memory **about** it.

Speaking from your own direct experience of the truth is different than speaking about someone else's direct experience. Both are still thought, but at lease one is direct. You may talk about somebody else's experience, and you may sound very pleasing and entertaining, but the truth is not yours. It is somebody else's. So have we established the difference between talking about the truth using someone's borrowed words and the other way of speaking from direct experience? One way is your own, it is direct. The other way is merely telling a story based on secondhand words. My friend Henry Maas has a saying:

**A belief is something we teach ourselves.
A myth is something we teach others.**

With that in mind I would like to tell you my experience. Before I wrote any of these thoughts down, I made a discovery that took me twelve years to realize its depth and truth. It was a very simple fact: I could see things differently if I wanted to. Simple, right? That was my discovery. I had an experience of the phrase:

Turn the other cheek

The reason it took me so long to really understand and assimilate this into my life was because I had incredible resistance to its simple truth. Things really **are not** what they seem. There is always another way to see the truth of something. We are very conditioned, though. We have had our minds trained to believe that a particular form of the truth is somehow better, or "more of" the truth than another form. The content is still the same, but the form is very different.

Are you after the **content** of the truth or just the

form because some "forms" tend to be more palatable than others? For instance, if you were told you could hear the Word of God at a particular church that was different than your own, and that the Truth about everything would be revealed, would you go? Probably yes. So let's say that you arrived at this new church where the Word of God was going to be revealed in all Its glory, but there were no pews. Instead, there were individual cubicles. And they had glass tops. And once inside you had to wear earphones. This cubicle is soundproof so you cannot hear anything but the Word, directly from God. The cubicles are also vision proof, making it so you cannot see anyone else in the church in order that you will not be distracted. After all, you want to hear **God**, right? You did not go to this church to hear the baby crying in the background during the sermon, right? At this church you would only hear and see God directly, theoretically. Would you go to this church? It would be very different from your own because you would not be allowed to see anyone else, hear anyone else, feel anyone else's presence except the direct presence of God. Would you go? (This is a rhetorical question.) My point is this: how much of church-going is for having a direct experience of God and how much of it has turned into a business of spiritual entertainment?

Are you transformed? Ever? And if you are transformed, why do you keep going back – do you forget that you were transformed? If you tell me that going to church is for the "reminder" then I ask you: are all these reminders dependent upon using memory? If so, then you are expected to remember the melody of the hymns so you sing the right notes. Memory expects you to pray the correct way, not forgetting to bow your head. But if you are required to use memory, why is it selective? You seem to forget everything you ever learned about God and continue to sin. Is salvation ever final? Why not? What is the point of returning to church every week if you merely forget what was said, ignore it, fall asleep in those god-awful **hard** pews, and live the rest of the week totally living **outside** of the "Word?" If you only experience God in the church, then the church means nothing anymore because all of us should then live in one big church and stop parading as heathens, heretics, and hypocrites in the world. We could never leave the church; we would be totally dependent upon it for its "ideas" about reality. If the message of church is to spread the message into the world, then you are using your memory again! Have you forgotten who you are? I think so. You can make direct contact without needing someone intervening for you. It is called: "Know thyself."

A lot of what people do is spiritual entertainment. It feels good. You get to meet other "God's children." Why are God's children only in **your** church? Why is your religion the correct one and mine wrong? Maybe I go to that church with the cubicles and the direct line to God…how do **you** know?! Can you begin to see the inherent problems in assuming that **your** way is the only way and all the others are merely silent gas emissions? I hope you begin to see the truth of:

"Judge not, thou be not judged."

It just means that if you judge somebody else, you

will feel as if **you** are being judged. It deals with the law of projections. Whatever you think about somebody else, you think about yourself also. If you speak from the highest in you, the highest in the other will answer. If you speak from the defender in you, the other person will defend himself, and no communication or transformation takes place. We will do anything to evade the present moment. We will do anything our clever brains can come up with to blow the opportunity for peace. It is not that peace does not exist except for church going people. It is rather that peace is coming at us at every moment and we blow the opportunity to realize it.

Shut up with all your complaining! Choose again. The wise person accepts things as they are. Whatever is not of truth will fall away. Whatever is not of love cannot hurt you. Only love is real, only love is eternal. If you have any pain – psychically or physically – you are not at peace with yourself and you are not rid of fear. A heart attack is a definite sign of someone who needs to wake up and smell the love that was always there, but they were probably too busy fearing life rather than loving it. They were probably too busy enabling their sick illusions instead of being at peace. No wonder people's bodies shut down – they don't love them, take care of them, or trust in their own miraculous powers of healing and self-renewal. The body cannot be sick, only the mind. The mind controls the body and not the other way around. Find out if you don't believe me. After all, it's your body.

My past taught me not to trust the present because the present moment was silent, lacking all thought, and thus all input of information, and opinions. The present is not an idea, it is a state of being. It is a silent, and in that silence is peace. It is an awareness that is directly connected to the universe. It is the "direct line" to God. So we cannot say that we "know" the present or that we "know" peace because peace is a state of being, it is who you are. It is not a word, it is not a memory. God is not a word. God is not the physical book of the Holy Bible. That is merely paper and ink. I do not think God is that small, nor does God come in editions and reprints. Do you think God would want to be "leather-bound?"

All my opinions, beliefs, prejudices, knowings and substitutes for love were challenged. It seemed as if they rallied against me when I had this epiphany. Like a seed, its influence in my life grew and grew. That seed is still growing today. I had the realization of "I can see things differently if I wanted to." The discovery was not of the statement itself, but the truth behind it. Its fact and truth "were," "is," and always "will be." The only problem was, I did not believe it. It took me twelve years to "see" it.

I tested the mysterious statement in various ways. How was I to know if it was true? It was not my experience, but just a sentence. It sounded very cool, like some New Age twist of ancient wisdom. Yet here I was – on the brink of discovering the meaning of life once and for all. But I still did not believe it. I was full of anger and rage and always thought the world was attacking every single effort I made on trying to bring peace to it. It was "little me" against the world. Those are not good odds, mind you. And I was a Generation Xer, and we were not supposed to believe anything. All that media hype was dead wrong. The media hype is always dead wrong. That is why it is called "hype." If it were self-evident and obvious, why is the hype necessary? Because it sells. But that is another book.

I continued testing the meaning of that phrase, getting into all kinds of mischief. Some results were disastrous, others were wonderful. Overall, I would say that making the shift from "seeing through a glass darkly" to "seeing through a glass lightly" (or at least seeing a glass full of Starbucks Mocha Frappuccino) was dramatic and traumatic. Looking back, I am baffled to realize how "out of it" I really was. I might **still** be "out of it" but at least now I am closer than I was. Now I have friends on the same path of peace. It was tough to be alone in my defensiveness toward the world conspiracy theory.

I used to be highly ambitious in areas that I did not even enjoy. It was useless ambition. Empty competition. I was in a race against nobody but myself. So if no one was competing, why was I always the loser? I was also highly productive, or so it seemed. I got good grades, took advanced classes, went to great universities. (Notice the plural? I think I kept switching undergraduate schools because: "The truth can't only be **here**, can it?")

I was young! I wanted to "explore the world!" I wanted to meet new people, expel "old friends," and really get on with it. I wanted to go out and "get a life," like it was at a store or something. What I was really doing was evading responsibility and escaping truth. If ever there was a "dark way," that was it. I was lost. I was depressed. And most of all, I was pissed that God was keeping something from me. As if he would. Here I was, waiting for God, when actually God was waiting for me. But remember: I did not need God, much less believe in God. I was a "Generation X." We have no beliefs, remember? No morals either. No life either. Those are all false for Generation X as well as Generation Y. Most of us look at the predominant world view as an infestation of adult-superiority, politically-corrupt, greedy-lawsuit-hungry-psycho-tv-watching, job-hopping, stock-market-gambling freaks, anyway. Excuse me. "Peace? Are you here someplace? Do I really have to PAY to have you?"

Only an imbecile would think the media is not influential despite its catering to the lowest common denominator of the human condition. This country lives for entertainment of the lesser, lower-level kind. The predominant choices are awful (if you must choose). And when youth are surrounded by it at every turn in everyday life, it tends to have its effects. Get out of your university research libraries and actually live the life of a teenager trying to find "the way," (or any way, for that matter) and find out how difficult it is to avoid all the crap that some adults make, and see how you like it! The children and teenagers and young adults are not in charge of the TV networks, the movie studios, the radio stations, the magazines, the video games, the gun shows, all that stuff. You adults ram it down our throats, with all your stupid advertising. Get over yourselves. If you want peace so badly, why not quit your job and go meditate on a cold rock in the Himalayas. At least you will be away from us – and take your noise and violence with you.

Anyways…

(I'll step off the soapbox for a few more paragraphs)

So I was empty. (Well isn't everyone?) That was what

it felt like. There was no one to talk to. They were all too busy with their jobs, their schedules, their "whatever." I had a sneaking suspicion that we were all thinking the same things, though. But nobody was saying it. All of us felt like there was more to life than the job, the routine, all the spiritual fads popping up. Religion was turned into the "flavor of the week." A friend and I went church hopping, instead of bar hopping. How Un-Generation X of us. How anti-establishment. How against the system we were. How deviating from our cool peers we were. At least we felt like we were getting somewhere. Had you ever noticed how unpopular some people become after they tell everyone else that they should not live in such a narrow moral universe; that they should live in a much broader one... like yours?

It got to the point that putting on the obligatory smile became impossible. I would look at other people and marvel at how they could possibly be living "happily ever after" when my life was such a mess because I was on a mission to discover the truth of some dumb insight, like:

"I could choose another way to see this."

I was not in "happily ever after." All I felt was impending doom now that I had discovered some secret statement, some key to the truth, some little shred of evidence that my life was supposed to have meaning and happiness in it. If only I knew where to shop for it. I had read every self-help book on the shelf. I tried being in different religions. When that didn't work, I tried just "being" instead. It felt like I was getting closer to something...

what that was I had no idea. My search felt deep and productive, though. In reality I was still deluding myself. Progress? Nope. Exalting oneself is just as wrong as undermining oneself.

It was like I was in Greenland trying to get to God at the North Pole, except I was going down via the South Pole and then coming back up north. I knew I was on a path, but I didn't think it would take so long. This was too much work. Was it worth it to find God? What if He was a She? What if I had to pay? What if my religion was the wrong one? What if "God—the Movie" was no longer showing on that holy movie screen called "my nice, separate, little Christian view of the world" (a screen on which "images" are "projected"... get it?)

I was no longer sure if I wanted to be so holy so fast. Maybe later on. I needed to work for a while and make a few bucks, get a savings account, go to school. I wanted to do ANYTHING but find God. Anything but... peace.

Such was my resistance to "letting go." But nothing seemed to be working. I tried learning Sanskrit and Hebrew. I read the Holy Bible, the Tao Te Ching, the Upanisads, the Bhagavad Gita, books by C.S. Lewis, tons of Jewish and Buddhist books. I read books on Hinduism, Islam, Sufism, Zen, yoga, Ayurveda, herbs, and chakras. I attended workshops, bought tapes, watched videos, got counseling, tried therapy...I even became best friends with one lady who just happened to be a psychologist. Leah Cooper was great. She used to say, "God Shmod. Just be real and follow the truth! It doesn't matter what the form is. We get distracted by all that stuff in front of the truth." She was right.

I took her advice seriously. Then I finally took myself seriously, for once. That was when I hit the bottom. Why? Probably because I was admitting to myself everything I had been blocking out for so long. I got real. I became honest with myself. And you know what happened? It hurt like hell! Why, oh why, was everything getting worse?! I thought I was spiritual! I thought I was doing all the spiritually-correct things! Why was my happiness being denied? Well, it was because I was denying it by constantly looking into the dark to figure out how to fix the dark. The only way to fix the dark is to turn on the light. So I bought one of those full-spectrum lights to help heal seasonal depression. Talk about stupid. It was just one more way of resisting the final step: total release, total surrender to God. I made some progress by giving God about 98 percent of my life, to do with it what He willed.

That extra 2 percent was definitely not His department, though. It was all my really dark stuff. It was the stuff I thought would make God throw up. As if God couldn't handle the little details of my life. We think we have to purify ourselves before we face God, thinking we can avoid grossing Him out. This is false and ridiculous. God IS the purifier so just let Him have it all. Give God your best shot. I do not think God looks at you and says: "Gee, I'd like to help you but your problems are too big for Me." We don't ask God for too much, we ask for too little.

Like many others before me, I threw my life up in the air: all my beliefs, bad habits, secrets, mistakes, greed, problems, insecurities, arrogance, my "whatever." I even went the extra step this time and "gave up" my very life and soul. Hey, I was on a roll. And I mean literally! I was rolling around on the floor in physical pain, sobbing my eyes out: "God, take it ALL! Take it ALL!!"

This time the prayer was real. It was no longer an intention or an empty promise. I meant it. I would have to be my word since God was going to be His word.

This prayer had conviction, willingness, incredible emotion, and gut-wrenching passion. It felt like I was going to die if I did not get all of it out. It went straight up to God. It went completely vertical, as the Eastern religions say. After twenty-eight years of praying, this was the first time it was Absolute because I renounced everything. This time it was real. This time, I felt "heard."

This time I had the willingness and the "space" to listen to the Response. The truth is, He was always there for me, I just did not believe it because I could not "see" it. But I was messed up on the semantics of "seeing." I thought it meant that I had to use my eyes. On the contrary, I do need my eyes to navigate in time and space, but I had to look even deeper by "seeing" with my open heart and having a mind open in order to have God "enter." Most people believe they have had an "experience" that was so earth-shattering, life-changing, mind-altering, and light-filling that the only way to describe it is to say they were "touched by the hand of God." Well, God definitely reached out and touched someone that day....... and it was me!

We have many names for people who are "not spiritual." Some of you may recognize them: Type-A personality, a real go-getter, fighter, maverick, tough-minded, atheist, agnostic, non-believer, democrat, republican, liberal, conservative, winner, champion, hero, star, leader, manager, boss, CEO, employee of the month, all-American, the boy next door. Do you know anyone like that? I was a few of those names.

Here are some others: depressed, lost, insane, delusional, hypocritical, over-worked, underpaid, stressed, hyperactive, hypochondriac, hypercritical, extra sensitive, anxious, nervous, genius, slow, secular, religious, self-righteous, selfish, charitable, and desperate. There are many names to describe someone who may or may not truly believe in a higher power. They just go through the motions, get by, and then find their life, coming down on top of them like a ton of bricks. Why does everything come crashing down if we are doing everything the world says is right? Well, because the "world" is our perception of it projected back to us. We only think we "see" it first, without us really deciding what we want to see first, and then we look at it and call it reality. We decide what we want our life to look like and the universe just says, "Okay, here it is, just what you ordered." In this life, whether we like it or not—whether we know it or not—we get what we paid for.

Do not kid yourself. Did it ever occur to you that you actually will your illnesses and problems to "happen" because at some level you feel a lack of love? It is true. Again, if you do not believe me then go find out for yourself. Do not take my word for anything. You discover the truth of it.

After getting down on my knees I stopped sobbing long enough to listen and wait. All was silent. Not one muscle moved. During what was one of the holiest moments in my life, I felt neither holy nor relieved. I was terrified.

Renouncing everything I knew about the world, I bet that everything I had – and knew – was going to be taken away from me. This was the first time I had acknowledged the existence of an intelligence greater than my own, small, belief-bound brain. It was the first time that I thought there might be more than the possibility that perhaps there may be a God….maybe. Sort of. Okay, so I was freaking out.

Now I was ready to discover the truth of: "see it differently." At this point I was seeing everything VERY differently, and my eyes were closed. I just listened. I waited. Very slowly, in the distance, I could begin to hear the faint songs of birds outside. Then I could hear children laughing in the apartment below me. I could smell the leftover scent of fabric softener on my sweat-soaked shirt. I could smell my sweat. Trembling, I opened my eyes. I think it was the first time I was really totally present. Kneeling in my own living room, I looked around. For about five seconds I recognized absolutely nothing.

Then memory kicked in and thoughts started rushing through my brain. If that is what a revelation feels like, then I definitely had one. I got the VERY CLEAR message that I was still alive and for a very good reason. My time was not done, yet. When you have an experience like this, you look back at your past and wonder why you were so upset over what now seems like the most mundane things. I was not upset for the reason I thought.

All I knew was that I was still alive in my apartment, the past was dead and gone, the future was all in my head, and for the first time in my life I felt "watched over." I was no longer upset, frantically trying to make my life happen. Many things became very clear. Worrying no longer existed. Fear was far, far away like the most distant star in the sky. Oh I remembered fear, but only because I still had a memory. We need the memory or else we could not survive. But we do not need fear, despite what a lot of books say. "Needing" fear is a ridiculous idea, because all of us already have plenty of it to go around. Who needs more of it? What we think we lack is the love to give to another, or the space to allow love into our hearts. This belief must be reversed if we are ever to be at peace.

I suppose some of you are wondering if I heard a voice, an angel, or even the Word of God, Himself. Well, for me it was a little different. I was always very skeptical of all that stuff like channeling spirits, psychic "readings" and the like… even though I explored those ideas and found them fascinating. But something about them did not totally jive with me. I guess I was similar to the people who say they do not believe in God: maybe they are just as skeptical as I was because they have not had an "experience" yet. My experience, or insight, or whatever you want to call it, was definitely "real" for me. In other words, the form may not be very believable as to the way it happened, but the content in the experience changed me.

The experience transformed me. And I think that is the point anyway. And I am not at all sorry that I cannot prove what happened. But then, the laws of Truth do not have to answer to the legal system of this country with all its lawyers. Lawyers can lose their "case" while Truth never loses anything.

Here is what my mind "heard" after I came out of

the momentary silence. It was not a "voice." Rather, it was a kind of "sense" that came to me in the form of words. It was like a confirmation of everything I had always known but it had gotten so buried deep inside my memory and soul, that it seemed as if I had forgotten it. When I "heard" it, it was like listening for the very first time. I did not react to it, but I grabbed a pen and wrote it down instead. Here it is:

First I felt a question coming from far away. It was very subtle and calm. It was not insisting. It calmly waited for me to acknowledge it. The question was: "Do you want to see?" A few seconds passed... then another question was floating there: "Why not?" Before I could answer what was probably a rhetorical question, the "answer" or "reply" started coming into my mind:

"Everything is laid out before you. It will open up before you and transform your mind. You can transcend time. It will awaken you. You have to listen in order to make the connection—for the infinite will be seen by many or few depending not on who desires, but who has the knowing to heed. The direction set forth has no limits. No earthly boundaries are attached to it, nor limited by it, can contain it, withhold it. Scrupulous care will be given to those who realize communication with this place is necessary for involvement in the whole. Nothing is finite but all is one. This is not the plan but the unfolding of Truth.

At this level you may not see if for long periods of what you call time. It must not be used for your means but only for Mine. You cannot be ruled and know freedom. Ideas of thought never transcend the power which is Everywhere. Your thoughts are small while a union of everyone is near a threshold of forgiveness. Forgetfulness is not a sin but wrong mindfulness is not either. You are moving towards awakening while many hear Me calling. This force is everywhere to consult with. It has no boundaries except the ones you have set upon it. Free your gates. Peace awaits you. Do your action. Falseness gets not Attention.

Life reveals itself to you in all facets. Can you see them? What shrouds your eyes does not cover Mine. I am withholding no mystery. Nor am I revealing everything. You will have what you need. I am with you, for I watch all, for eternity. Your comfort is My love and all Truth is in you. Nothing is lost, more is coming: to you it will take time as you know it. It is already done. You are very safe. Know I will comfort you.

Expansion is necessary and you are needed. What are you going to choose? I am a decision. The path that love takes does not involve calculation but an unfolding of the whole One to your mind. Be It to see It. It will reveal itself to you. Hold no beliefs, but Trust is necessary.

You will not remember what will happen as

your memory of the world serves no purpose but a lapse out of love into time. Do not seek, for it is coming at you without sound. You will not recognize it, for your memory is false. It will become you and you will think you "know" it. Do not try to put away the past for it is only memory running its course. If you are to be an Extension of the Will you need not forget what you already "know" but rather let go of your passion to control.

Whichever way you do turn, can you survive the past and build the future? Your foundation of hope turns misery to shame. There will not be lessons of pain for those who pay attention to the True Spirit of the Course. You have it – a will – to use at your disposal. But can you dispose of the Truth when it beckons you to call upon it? Your own layers melt away; discarding the present is impossible. It is always there when you are lapsed in memory. Do not stray. Your Path is chosen. You will do It."

All I could make out from that was that peace and happiness would be the inevitable result of living in the Truth. "Living happily ever after" would no longer be an elusive phenomenon. Abundance was no longer an idea discussed in a best-seller. Gentleness was no longer under a female monopoly. World Peace was no longer a bumper sticker advertising green, orb-like vegetables. Reality was no longer virtual – it was REAL!

What else did I understand from that little encounter with higher consciousness? I knew that "calm" was not only for the willow tree. I knew that "meaning" was no longer just a word in the dictionary. In short, it seemed "I" had arrived. I still wonder about that.

I perceived life very differently. I no longer asked questions like: "How much money do I need?" or "What clothes are the best?" or "What do I have to do to be cool or sophisticated?" or "Who should I date now?" or "What do I need in order to be successful, rich, powerful, and happy and still have great sex?" Those were questions from the past, from the "dark way."

I do not profess to be an enlightened master, by any means. However, I have noticed that I seem to be more at peace with myself. There is no more imbalance or warring going on between my thoughts and my actions. Is fear now impossible? I think so. I really think so. As long as I can still eat the chocolate cake once in a while, I will be just fine. You know what I mean.

My questions have changed, too. Now I ask things like: "How many good deeds could I perform if I was no longer busy defending my beliefs, fighting over opinions, and needing to be right?" I mean, just how peaceful are you when you defend your beliefs? No one defends unless one feels attacked.

If your "god" is watching over you and you actually believe that, why do you need to defend anything? Why do you need to defend your all-powerful god anyway? Our words are small compared to the power of God, are they not? Our opinions mean nothing in the face of the Truth, do they not?

If you truly believe in the awesome power of the Universe, the Greater Intelligence, are you at total peace with your conviction that you are safe? That you are watched over? Do you have faith that **nothing**—not even another's opinion "for" or "against" your god—can diminish God's power running through you, watching over you, guiding you, loving you? Do you have conviction, or do you perceive someone else's "experience" of God as heretical, thus "threatening" your religion? Are you that faithless? Do you think it is petty to defend one's religion? I mean, it is your opinion against their opinion….so who is the bigger fool, huh? If you merely agree with me or understand me those are still just ideas in your brain. Discover the silence of stillness. Discover that Truth is not a bunch of words.

Truth cannot be threatened by fear, evil, or anything that is in the realm of relative knowledge such as thoughts, opinions, and belief systems. Only the truth is real. We think that we need to defend our religion and belief system because somehow God gets His feelings hurt when someone believes in something different than what we believe. How do you know that? Did Jesus have breakfast with you and tell you so? I mean my experience was a little weird in itself, but so far I cannot find any point on which to argue with it. If it was real, I am fine. If not, I am still fine. Enjoy the following quotes on personal growth.

By degrees, little by little, from time to time,
a wise person should remove
his own impurities as a smith removes
the dross from silver.

Buddhism, Dhammapada 239

~

Muhammad is the Apostle of God;
and those who are with him are strong
against unbelievers, but compassionate
amongst each other....
And their similitude in the Gospel is:
Like a seed which sends forth its blade, then
makes it strong; it then becomes thick, and it
stands on its own stem, filling the sowers with
wonder and delight.

Islam, Qur'an 48.29

~

Every one to whom much is given,
of him much will be required.

Christianity, Luke 12.48

~

We rejoice in our sufferings, knowing that suffering produces endurance, and endurance produces character, and character produces hope, and hope does not disappoint us, because God's love has been poured into our hearts.

Christianity, Romans 5.3-5

~

Through constant effort over many lifetimes, a person becomes purified of all selfish desires and attains the supreme goal of life.

Hinduism, Bhagavad Gita 6.45

~

Study of Torah leads to precision, precision to zeal, zeal to cleanliness, cleanliness to restraint, restraint to purity, purity to holiness, holiness to meekness, saintliness to the holy spirit, and the holy spirit to life eternal.

Judaism, Talmud, Aboda Zara 20b

~

*God is on the watch for the nations of the
world to repent, so that He may bring
them under His wings.*

Judaism, Midrash, Numbers Rabbah 10.1

~

*The Dharma of the Buddhas by the constant
use of a single flavor causes the several worlds
universally to attain perfection, by gradual
practice all obtain the Fruit of the Way.*

Buddhism, Lotus Sutra 5

~

*Let every person ask pardon of the great
Light Asis, The Molder of us all.*

*African Traditional Religions
Kipsigis Tradition (Kenya)*

~

*Liberation is the best thing,
as the moon is best among the stars.*

Jainism, Sutrakritanga 1.11.22

~

Through your sojourn in the world,
Know your station in life.
Know it well, you in the world,
know it well.

Shinto, Moritake Arakida
One Hundred Poems about the World

~

Lord! You are the uninvoked savior, motiveless
compassionate being, a well-wisher even when
unsprayed, a friend even when unrelated.

Jainism, Vitaragastava 13.1

~

God is always impartial and compassionate.
At least three times he tries to lead even the
most wicked men (to salvation) by the way
of their minds.

Unification Church, Sun Myung Moon

~

*That disciplined man with joy and light
within, becomes one with God and reaches
the freedom that is God's*

Hinduism, Bhagavad Gita 5.24

~

*Your word is a lamp to my feet
and a light to my path.*

Judaism and Christianity, Psalm 119.105

~

*The truth has come, and falsehood
has vanished away. Surely falsehood
is ever certain to vanish.*

Islam, Qur'an 17.85

~

*Jesus spoke to them, saying, "I am the light of
the world; he who follows me will not walk in
darkness, but will have the light of life."*

Christianity, John 8.12

~

Proclaim liberty throughout the land
to all its inhabitants.

Judaism and Christianity, Leviticus 25.10

~

The fetters of the heart are broken, all doubts
are resolved, and all works cease to bear fruit,
when He is beheld who is both high and low.

Hinduism, Mundaka Upanisad 2.2.8

~

You will know the truth,
and the truth will make you free.

Christianity, John 8.32

~

No man is free,
but he who labors in the Torah.

Judaism, Mishnah, Abot 6.2

~

*Being in accord with the Tao,
he is everlasting.*

Taoism, Tao Te Ching 16

~

*No call to God can be unheard nor left
Unanswered. And of this I can be sure;
His answer is the only one I really want.*

*A Course in Miracles, Workbook
for Students, Lesson 358*

~

*That which is the finest essence—this whole
world that is the Self. That is reality.
That is the Self. That art thou.*

Hinduism, Chandogya Upanisad 6.8.7

~

*If I am not for myself who is for me?
And when I am for myself what am I?
And if not now, when?*

Judaism, Mishnah, Abot 1.14

~

All things exist for world peace.

Perfect Liberty Kyodan, Precept 14

~

Blessed are the peacemakers,
for they shall be called sons of God.

Christianity, Matthew 5.9

~

He brings together those who are divided,
he encourages those who are friendly;
he is a peacemaker, a lover of peace,
impassioned for peace,
a speaker of words that make for peace.

Buddhism, Digha Nikaya xiii.75, Tivija Sutra

~

God is peace, His name is peace, and all is
bound together in peace.

Judaism, Zohar, Leviticus 10b

~

*For whoever would save his life will lose it,
and whoever loses his life for my sake
will find it.*

Christianity, Matthew 16.25

~

*In the remembrance of God
do hearts find satisfaction.*

Islam, Qur'an 13.28

~

*If a man sings of God and hears of Him,
And let love of God sprout within him,
All his sorrows shall vanish,
And in his mind,
God shall bestow abiding peace.*

Sikhism, Adi Granth, Japuji 5, M.1, p.2

~

*Thou dost keep him in perfect peace,
whose mind is stayed on thee,
because he trusts in thee.*

Judaism and Christianity, Isaiah 26.3

~

If you wish to untie a knot,
you must first understand how it was tied.

Buddhism, Surangama Sutra

~

The Way out into the light often looks dark,
the way that goes ahead often looks as if it
went back. The way that is least hilly often
looks as if it went up and down. The virtue
that is really loftiest looks like an abyss, What
is sheerest white looks unsullied.

Taoism, Tao Te Ching 41

~

The sage awakes to light in the night
of all creatures. That which the world calls
day is the night of ignorance to the wise.

Hinduism, Bhagavad Gita 2.69

~

You are an extremely valuable, worthwhile significant person even though your present circumstances may have you feeling otherwise.

James W. Newman

~

You possess a potent force that you either use, or misuse, hundreds of times every day.

J. Martin Kohe

~

It is the mind that maketh good or ill, that maketh wretch or happy, rich or poor.

Edmund Spenser

~

Begin to be now what you will be hereafter.

St. Jerome

~

*Your behavior will match your picture
of yourself.*

Dorothy Corkille Briggs

~

*You stagnate in an uncommitted relationship
because you don't know how make
or ask for a commitment.*

Gay Hendricks

~

*How much of your talent is being wasted for
want of a little boldness?*

Drs. Tom Rusk and Randy Reed

~

*Success, or failure, very often arrives
on wings that seem mysterious to us.*

Dr. Marcus Bach

~

It is discipline that frees us.

Nellie Tholen

~

They always say that time changes things, but you actually have to change them yourself.

Andy Warhol

~

Take a music bath once or twice a week for a few seasons, and you will find that it is to the soul what the water-bath is to the body.

Oliver Wendell Holmes

~

We are here on earth to do good for others. What are others here for, I don't know.

W.H. Auden

~

You're still in the land of the living.
You're not dead yet –
so stop living as if you are!

Bette Midler in "Beaches"

~

Successful people don't care about "success."

David James

~

You have to leave the city of your comfort
and go into the wilderness of your intuition.
What you'll discover will be wonderful.
What you'll discover will be yourself.

Alan Alda

~

Fall seven times, stand up eight.

Japanese Proverb

~

If you don't know where you're going,
you'll probably end up somewhere else.

David Campbell

~

I can do it, I will do it,
I have to do it, I'm doing it…
I've done it!

Candia Engleman

~

Work… and do it with a sense of urgency.

Sandi McFerran

~

Most people are afraid to say what they want,
that's why they don't get what they want.

Madonna

~

Why are we on this Earth?
We're not just on this Earth to make other
people happy. We're here to be good, to help,
to make the world a better place.
I know that sounds really corny but
I'm 100% certain that we're not all put
on this Earth just so we can make lots of
money and be successful.
The only thing that matters in life
is loving people.

Madonna

~

All you people can't you see how your love's
affecting your reality?
Every time you're down you can make it right.
And that makes you larger than life.

Backstreet Boys

~

*Never doubt that a small group
of thoughtful, committed citizens
can change the world. Indeed,
it is the only thing that ever has.*

Margaret Mead

~

*To see a World in a Grain of Sand
And a Heaven in a Wild Flower,
Hold Infinity in the palm of your hand
And Eternity in an hour.*

William Blake

~

Wherever you turn is God's face.

Muhammad

~

The disciples said to him, "When will the
repose of the dead happen, and
when will the new world come?"
Jesus said, "What you are waiting
for has already come,
but you don't recognize it."

The Gospel of Thomas

~

There is an essential unity in all religions; there is no
difference in the truths inculcated by the various
faiths; there is but one method by which the world,
both external and internal, has evolved; there is but
one Goal admitted by all scriptures. But this basic
truth is one not easily comprehended. The discord
existing between the different religions, and the
ignorance of men, make it almost impossible to lift the
veil and have a look at this grand verity. The creeds
foster a spirit of hostility and dissension; ignorance
widens the gulf that separates one creed from another.
Only a few specially gifted persons can arise superior
to the influence of their professed creeds and find
absolute unanimity in the truths propagated by all
great faiths.

Swami Sri Yukteswar Giri, 1894

~

How happy are the poor in spirit:
their's is the kingdom of heaven.
Happy the gentle:
they shall have the earth for their heritage.
Happy those who mourn:
they shall be comforted.
Happy those who hunger and thirst for what is right:
they shall be satisfied.
Happy the merciful:
they shall have mercy shown them.
Happy the pure in heart:
they shall see God.
Happy the peacemakers:
they shall be called Sons of God.
Happy those who are persecuted in the cause of right:
their's is the kingdom of heaven.

Matthew 5:3-10, the Beatitudes

~

Are the Ideas in Scripture Real or Not?

Are the Ideas in Scripture Real or Not?

IDEAS ARE OPINIONS. Opinions are beliefs. Then beliefs are translated into words. Words use language. Language can be arranged into sentences esteemed to be codified "laws." Sometimes we call these laws "commandments." That last word can be classified under another word called "religion." The word "religion" uses the concept of the word "God." The word "God," however, is not the actual God. The word God has its meaning derived from the use and context of other words and ideas. But are any of the words, themselves, real?

Are the words and ideas of God timeless – having emerged from the changeless knowledge of eternity itself? Or are they *our* ideas projected onto God—our ideas which have always changed with the times? Are religious laws eternal or do they last only if we keep talking about them, hence religion's total dependence on language and its subjective meaning of words in order to pass along a belief system that has not always existed until the common-era (get it: *written* history)? What makes anything real or believable? Is an idea True just because a lot of people believe it? How do we judge what is true and what is false?

For those of you who are so advanced in the mystique of the human condition, who deem yourselves as already complete, whole, perfectly healthy, totally empowered, holy, sinlessly religious, always with joy, love, bliss, and in total communion with your higher Self, wisdom, angels and spirit guides… you can skip this chapter. In fact, just skip the entire book. (You're probably quoted in it from one of your past lives anyway.) But for the rest of us who have not yet learned how to read auras, throw the I Ching, consult the Oracle at Delphi, hold annual conversations with God just in time for the release of its published transcript (just in time for Christmas!), or quell our neighbors' craving for Holy Ganga, we are compelled to ask such illumined (great new age word) questions in order to: 1) feel better than we do now; 2) feel better than we did last night; or 3) sufficiently elevate our Emotional Spiritual Quotient so we can finally say with boldness and ennui, "I am seeking God. Get away from me you illiterate heathen."

Is it possible to live a moral and good life without a belief in God or by following a religion or a spiritual path? Is morality totally dependent upon the Absolute word of a god? Or has mankind invented this "Absolute" quality in order to claim that he is the channel, speaker, or messenger for God; thus giving himself the divine power to mete out punishment or reward as if he was the actual god? Sounds rather feudal and futile, doesn't it?

Perhaps mankind should leave all judgments to God, including judgments about morality. Have you read about how mercy is higher than judgment? In the book of James it says, "If you really keep the royal law found in Scripture, 'Love your neighbor as yourself,' you are doing right. But if you show favoritism, you sin and are convicted by the law as lawbreakers. For whoever keeps the whole law and yet stumbles at just one point is guilty of breaking all of it…. judgment without mercy will be shown to anyone who has not been merciful. Mercy triumphs over judgment." Amen!

Okay, folks. Let's point out something that most people seem to overlook about judgment … quite conveniently, I might add. This has to do with projection or, in other words, making something up.

For Democrats, Republicans, believers, nonbelievers, atheists, agnostics, liberals, and conservative moral absolutists alike (who claim that all morals and all things good are defined only by God as coming from God's absolute and inarguable "laws" – all of which all humans must follow or else be considered an abomination of God's will), I pose these questions:

How can anyone know that God is a good, absolute dictator of morality except by what is one's own completely infallible moral judgment, or, if you will, absolute and unerring perception that God is good enough to listen to, and therefore believe in and have faith in, in the first place?

*Must we rely on mere belief or faith in God in order to be considered moral and good, such that all nonbelievers in God – according to **"God's"** definition of what He is (and not our **own**, get it?) — are somehow immoral and living examples of abominations and deviants devoid of any worth and value?*

The flip side of not "needing" certain types of people who are often deemed an "abomination" or even "deviant" is that if we don't even NEED them, why would we even WANT them? Of course this means that we JUST need certain people no matter how much we don't really want them. So why not just get rid of them NOW by saving God some time by letting US judge them before GOD can, and thus avoid mercy altogether? Does this still sound very LOVING or MORAL to you? Or is it something else, akin to a fallible human being's personal agenda to spread one's own abominable judgments, belief system, and laws dictating what they think God's moral universe ought to be, according to human opinion?

It seems we can only see God as good if, at first, we have a sense of what it means to be good in the first place. Don't we – quite unavoidably – use our own moral insight to decide if God's "word" is good or even real? How would we know to heed? Why should we believe or ignore something that is said just because of who says it? If you don't want to believe what I am saying just because I am saying it, what makes God somehow more "believable" than anyone else just because God said so? How can we avoid making any projections whatsoever, here? Is it possible to "know" anything at all if we can only interpret everything we see according to what we would want it to be? These are serious and profound questions that require a deeper, further study. Ganga anyone?

And, no, I am neither condoning nor condemning the use of holy herb, here. My point is that we tend not to like anything that challenges or questions our beliefs. Some prefer to escape from deeper questions, seeking refuge in avoidance. Some people check out using drugs. Others think they're "checking in" by having faith, when perhaps it is nothing more than "checking out" under the guise of appearing pious and religious. We often fear our own questions, which means we fear ourselves. We have forgotten what judgment is for. We are supposed to "judge" for peace, not against it. We are supposed to choose love, the highest wisdom. Unfortunately, a lot of people insist on projecting onto god our wrath and fury, thus proving that fearing God is somehow rational, even real. This is one more way, one more excuse cloaked in biblical language, one more "reason," one more justification that we would rather choose fear over peace. This is insane.

It is also narcissistic. Some people never progress beyond the extreme need for love from someone else, a superficial social skill infants use out of basic instinct and a need to survive. Narcissists are deeply rooted in fear because they have never learned how to love another person, or themselves, without reservations or conditions. It is they who need to have conditions for love, and those conditions are defined by the narcissist as: "Love me my way, not your way."

Other people are not viewed as individuals of worth

or value unless their attention is focused entirely on pleasing the narcissist. Can you see a parallel, here, with fanatical people infected with the disease to please their god or their religion who never seem to reach "the peace that passeth understanding?" Peace is not pleasing to these people. They find their "peace" when they can control everything, which can only mean that they are not at peace to begin with. Uncertainty spells certain death in hell for the narcissist. Control means heaven. Everything must serve the needs of the narcissist. Everyone must satisfy the needs and desires of the narcissist because the narcissist has no feeling of self-worth. He has no sense of self-love. He has no sense of right judgment, and therefore judges against others who do not give him the excessive, unearned respect that he demands. The result is a person (or god, for that matter) who is easily hurt, who reacts with vengeance, wrath, fury, rage, seeking the annihilation of the "problem" in whatever manner necessary, up to and including termination. This "god" must go if we are to judge in favor of peace, in favor of letting go of our collective and narcissistic fears.

Kai Nelson is a professor of philosophy at the University of Calgary, Alberta, Canada. He claims in his book, "Ethics Without God," that we must first judge for ourselves the moral quality of any revelation, law, or commandment purporting to be the unerring word of god. We make the first judgment because we have an internal yardstick by which we invariably measure our ability to heed anyone's words. Otherwise we would not know whether it was good to continue listening to and heeding the words of what the god said, and then believe that particular god as being good just because the god said He was good.

Perhaps we have judged god first all along. It may be that we can't handle our own personal power yet. Thus we made god, religion, spirituality, and our own self-image into the great cosmic garbage cans into which we dump all our problems without ever facing them ourselves. For some of us on the path, we cannot handle the responsibility or accountability it takes to shine brightly from a sense of healthy self-love. Some people are still stuck in their own self-made hells of narcissistic tendencies. To them, life is hell and other people are hell. Little do they know that they made it that way. Their attack thoughts are inside their own minds, not the mind of the person in front of them from whom they seek the love only they can give to themselves. This kind of victim is self-made.

Some people hate themselves and then project that self-hatred onto others, blame them, and then hold them accountable for all the so-called "problems" in the world. In essence such people claim, "You are bad, but I am good...all because my god said so. And because you are ruining my world, god will punish you." Yet, not facing our true selves can be the only and greatest of all sins, the greatest opportunity to blow the chance for inner peace.

Sometime this vicious cycle of projection and narcissism has to end. It can end only when we start with ourselves, first. Instead of asking, "What am I not getting," we need to ask, "What am I not giving?" Leave the others alone because you have enough to do without taking on someone else's problems. Start with yourself. Choosing the path of wisdom means choosing the highest judgment of the good kind, the loving kind, the wise kind. Place yourself in the arms of the universe and let it decide for you. Make no decisions by yourself today, without consulting wisdom first. Relax into a judgment higher than your own. Judgments against ourselves, and others, are more distorted than not. Can we avoid bad judgments entirely? Why or why not?

How, but through human judgment (which we know is fallible) can we know the difference between what purports to be revelation and what is in fact revelation? People cannot avoid using their own judgment, ideas, perceptions, and opinions when it comes to: 1) deciding whether or not they will listen to a god that speaks commandments; and then 2) following that commandment not because people first thought it was "good" or "real," but because God said so first. Is this god full of universal love and wisdom, or just your own limited, selective love?

Whether you like it or not, whether you want to believe it or not, people judge first whether or not they will follow a god's commandments. Our own judgment of morality can be the only logical prior experience in any situation otherwise we would not have the discrimination to know whether or not we should believe in, follow, listen to, heed and obey any god. It almost sounds like a loophole in the "free will" argument, yes? God reports, and then we decide. Just like Fox News. Do you think God would stand up against the O'Reilley Factor? Make sure your answer is pithy when you give it, otherwise no mercy for you!

Are believers who claim they never question god

(because to do so would be blasphemy) only kidding themselves, not realizing that in making such a claim they, too, have pre-judged god to be "good" and "real" in order that they may believe in God? Think about it. Is this really a matter of the "chicken and the egg" type of thing? Is this whole argument even worth having if it means activating the brain all the more, ensuring that we never experience inner peace? Ah ha! Did you ever think about it that way? Do you *really* want inner peace, or do you want to defend something, some idea, or some belief?

Has this provoked you into thinking beyond the mere words of a scripture and discovering the truth of the words for yourself? Or will you just accept your opinion about all beliefs as being totally devoid of judgment before you listened to and followed your one God? Are you sure you have that "mercy," too? Are you beyond narcissism? How would you know?

Don't get upset over this, please. These are mere words printed with ink. You need only consider what your mind is going into right now, after reading all this. Are you currently experiencing "the peace that passeth understanding?" Why or why not? Do you still want to hold on to your opinion about morality and judgment as being the only "right" way? Are you attached to your spirituality? Where is the freedom in that? How absolute is that? Be honest with yourselves.

Don't settle for some phony opinion or idea no matter how "religious" it may or may not be. A lot of people deceive themselves by hiding all their prejudices or problems cloaked and draped in religious language, as if mere terminology and words are sufficient for proving or disproving reality. Do not hide behind your ideas about what you think is real – find out if your faith is strong, if it is true, if you are living your "word" or if you are just faking it out of some "fear of the Lord." Because that is NOT faith. That is NOT wisdom. That is ignorance based on your opinion, and this ignorance has ruled mankind forever. Wake up!

Ideas are opinions which are beliefs made up of words from a particular language. When you organize those ideas into a specific set of codified rules—arbitrarily set by a human being wishing to control the thoughts of others—then you have commandments and laws. These make up another set of ideas (remember that ideas come from language and words) called Religion. In order for no one to argue with religion, we say that some deity with powers greater than us has the final say in what is true and what is false, what is good and what is bad. Religion relies upon a particular set of words that we use in order to communicate.

First there was the word. Words come from language. If you can control the language that is being spoken, you can control the thoughts that people think. Therefore it is valid to say that religion is a form of mind control or thought control. If the word "God" is removed from a conversation or a train of thought or even an entire language, does God still exist? If not, are the ideas and language mechanisms used to describe a power greater than us (one that we have never seen or heard from recently) being used? When language alters or changes, by definition the thoughts of the people who use the language changes.

The human being is not born with an innate concept of a particular type of God. The Catholics talk about the Virgin Mary and some claim they can see Her. The Muslims worship Muhammad and Allah, and their visions follow accordingly. The Christians talk about their kingdom of heaven and Jesus is in it. The Hindus talk about Shiva and… well… I don't want to get into that because there are too many arms.

We are taught to use the vocabulary of whatever religion we were raised with and its intrinsic ideas just as we are taught the vocabulary and stories of Greek mythology. This does not make them true. Greek Gods do not exist even though they have names. The Christian God allegedly exists, but is that existence true only because the concept of God exists only in a word in the form of a name?

Why are we are conditioned to fear God, our "Creator?" How can we fear a word? For one thing, we have given a name to this power that is greater than us. When something has a name it seems more tangible, more controllable, more real. Just like calling certain people "abominations" or biological mistakes. Does that make them so? The assigning of a name *can* trigger our fear of it—especially when we do not understand what is beyond the mere label of a name. Especially when we judge before God judges. Some people just *love* to play God. Had you noticed?

We have attached so much significance to "holy" words, that we feel (not "think," because thinking involves reasoning, logic, and a modicum of actual experience and observation) certain words have some physical, existential meaning beyond the actual written word. Words have no life. They are symbols. Ideas have no life beyond our brains. They are images in our heads. Nevermind the quantum physics and chemistry of it all, because we all *know* that if we were meant to explore life in scientific or secular terms only, then surely God would have told us to go for it, right? Wrong? If you're about to settle for an idea here, watch out! Your understanding would be a misunderstanding. Interpretations are only <u>about</u> reality.

"First there was the word" describes the origins of divine, creative language which we attribute to "God" because God's language is the language of creation. If you do not use this "language" properly then you get screwed up in the world. Remember the Tower of Babel? If you do not follow one person's religion (as defined by the particular culture's language) then you are considered "outside" that religion. You are outside that realm of ideas and thought. If you merely do not share the same belief about the particular meaning of word as other people do in a particular religion, are you bad? I challenge any Christian to define "God" without using circular reasoning, without defining God in terms of religious language. Can it be done? Can we define God without using scriptures? Why or why not? Be honest. Make sure your conclusions and ideas are from your own experience, and not someone else's borrowed words. Be honest in your absoluteness, if possible.

Is God merely a word drummed up by some ancient church authority who used language to indoctrinate ignorant people—people who did not have command over the language the way the clergy did because the ignorant were merely uneducated? Possibly. "God" became just another word, another idea.

At this point you may be getting upset. You want to defend your belief system! You want to defend the meaning of a word. This may be happening because you have been conditioned to *defend* your ideas and belief systems. They depend on using certain words that are specifically defined by your own narrow scope of imagination or knowledge of actual history. God is an idea designated to be "sacred" by the history of the church and religion. In reality you cannot fear words, themselves, because by themselves they mean nothing.

Words have meaning only in some larger context. The Church has defined that context in terms of good versus evil, punishment and reward, sin versus salvation, and man against God, man against himself, and man against the world. Can you see how the church has done a wonderful job at making life seem utterly futile if we look at the overwhelming odds against us?

Why are we conditioned to believe that anything (especially life) is against us? Uh, *hello!* That sounds like narcissism again! Throughout history man has fought nature rather than live in harmony with it. Man is always trying to control life rather than let it be. The church has tried to control man by indoctrinating him to become more dependent upon the power of the church rather than become dependent on the power of a wise, unconditionally loving God (i.e.: "Love people according to *our* way, not *your* way" or "pray *our* way, not *your* way.") The power of God is available everywhere, not just from the mouth of the seemingly never-satisfied, control-hungry, power mongering, narcissistic church. The church has never been at peace with the world. Yet people worship the church's example as the way to peace. This is one reason why we are not at peace. We worship insanity and narcissism and yet we don't even know it. Maybe we don't want to.

Who has the wisdom to see the paradox? Who has the wisdom to see beyond the illusions of a "holy" church when it does nothing more than inhibit the natural flow of the universe with its constricting dogma choking the life out of everything that defines what it means to be fully alive and fully human? What could be more sacred than to be fully alive as a human being who just "IS?" Will we ever be free from the ties in which religion has us bound? Is there any truth to fighting the ways of nature? In nature, in reality, there is no right or wrong. Those are manmade concepts exploited by religion. The question is, how do we want to live: in peace or in constant disagreement, fear, war, and fighting over opinions—which means not being at peace? We have to look at the system of communication called "language" for some clues.

Is religion intrinsic to human nature or is it imposed on us through the church's manipulation and control over language? How can religion be passed on except by language? Think about it. Rewrite the dictionary or any scripture by removing the word God, and see if people who have never had the idea of God (on their own) try and come up with it themselves. Try it. It does not work. Do you know why? Because one of the functions of the church throughout history has been to perpetuate a thought system that is afraid of updating knowledge, history, and language. The church is literally afraid of certain "words."

Congregations were not supposed to have control

over the meaning of words and the use of language. The church derived its power by instituting the "need" for a preacher or a prophet of God to interpret language for others. In doing so, the church secured a constant flow of new members who had to be totally dependent upon the church to interpret the "true" meaning of God's words. Who wouldn't go? Back then if you were not "smart enough" to be able to discover the "love for the word of God" on your own, you were blasphemous, a horrible sinner, and in serious need of the church's "help" so they could save you (or execute you).

"Church" became a huge business—like much of it is today. God sells as well as sex sells. What is more, the church *knows that* and still uses guilt to bring people in who are afraid of normal sexual feelings that are merely nothing more than that: feelings. It was the church that defined that certain feelings are bad while others are good. The church has always controlled the meaning of life out of a fear of it. If no one feared the Lord, we would not need the church. And that is *exactly* what the church does not want to happen. The church cannot survive if all of us find peace. Who would be left to judge? Who would we hate and fear? Where would we direct our prejudice? Who would we blame for society's problems?

What if YOU became the biblical scholar and discovered for yourself that the history of religion has been one of the most violent, non-peaceful, evil storylines ever created... by *man*? "Thou shalt not kill" has killed more people in the name of God than anything else.

The church has used its power to control language, to transmit God's "word" according to its own prejudiced, biased, judgmental, "jealous and wrathful" views. The church created "God" in OUR image, and not the other way around. We believe that God is jealous, wrathful and judgmental because WE are jealous, wrathful, and judgmental.

During the middle ages the church controlled who received an education. Ignorant people who knew nothing of the horrific murders the church was committing were very easily swayed to "believe" in the "benevolent" power of the church. The same is true today. Some churches have continued to indoctrinate people out of *fear*. This way they can manipulate and control people's thoughts using fear, guilt, hatred, prejudice and anger.

I ask you: is this the way to teach people about peace and love? Or is it just a way to persuade, influence, and sway people into becoming totally dependent upon the church for a steady stream of prejudiced dogma because people can no longer take it upon themselves to see love in the person in front of them? Why have we become so deaf to our own inner voice of truth that IS the truth of God? We have lost confidence in ourselves. We have lost sight of self-reliance. We have lost sight of peace. Using fear as a control mechanism for thought control is called *the history of religion.*

Remove any of the fearful, angry, prejudiced, hateful emotions from any pulpit and see if the preacher can give a peaceful sermon. Is it impossible to preach religion these days without condemning somebody else, especially ourselves?

What if religion meant loving everybody equally? Religion, as we know it, would die. Today's religion in the church is based on fear and the exclusion of anyone who does not speak its own narrow language, based on out-dated language uses of syntax, vocabulary, and context. Have someone read the bible and tell you exactly what it means and you will see that for each person on the planet, there is a different interpretation. No wonder the church insists on controlling the "meaning" of the bible. God forbid if people actually had to read it themselves and see the message of universal love written all over it!

If you read the bible, try replacing the word "God" with the word "language," and you will read it entirely differently. Try substituting the idea of language, words, and context for the word "God" and you will begin to see that the bible is also a written explanation for the birth of the written word as a way to control people's thoughts using fear, guilt, superstitions, and the threat of death. The church—as history proves—has justified, in the name of God, excluding or killing people who do not follow its rules, dogma, and message of fearing another human being.

That is not the message of love, forgiveness, authentic power, or joy. In short, excluding anyone from God's love is not the message of the Holy Spirit. The church is losing its suffocating control over the use and meaning of language because people are waking up to the larger, more realistic, more joyous message of universal love—which is the ultimate message of Christ, the Holy Spirit, God, and Jesus. The Ultimate Truth is Love, a truth over which no human construct of thought or language can possibly contain or control. God is infinite, *we are not*. God is love, and it is our mission to follow Him. Jesus was an example of *how* to walk the path. We can no longer say that happiness, peace, and loving one another is impossible. It is possible to love everyone rather than fearing them. Love, inclusion, forgiveness, and truth are the ways to which we must turn. We need to do it now.

It is not my opinion but a fact that words are words no matter where they are and who writes them. Words are mere symbols of reality, not reality itself. No one entity, like the church, can control the Ultimate Reality. We were not created to look at life and then live it completely backwards, according to what we think. We are supposed to be living life according to how God thinks, or how He wants us to live. We need to watch life for clues on how to be. It is wrong-minded thinking ("sin") to try and control God's creation, according to narcissism and not by love.

The only reason you get upset when someone calls you a name, or challenges your belief system is because you have identified your life and very being with the meaning of those words. Your identity literally IS the word. However that is only your perception and not reality. Remember that "sticks and stones can break my bones but names can never hurt me?" How quickly we find religion scattering about trying to defend its "words" as representing the only reality. How quickly the authoritative church can threaten us by making up stories about God coming down and killing someone for not following His "words." I think the church feels more threatened by the constant change of society more than God does. He has better things to do than to worry about fearful images of mass destruction—*and so do we.* Why do we waste so much of our time worrying about life rather than living it in joy? We are afraid of mere words.

God is not a word. God is an idea, and ideas are based on beliefs. What is a life form? Is life a belief or an idea? Life is real; it is actual. Nature is real. The action of life does not need language in order to survive. But ideas need language in order to survive. Otherwise they do not exist. Does God exist? The idea of God is false but the reality of God is real. In other words, the mere idea of God is not actually "God." Argue all you want, but try not using the concept of language to define or explain God and you will fail miserably. We have made God a "word," and that's all. God's infinite power and love can hardly be contained in words. Not one manmade entity can have a monopoly on God; not even religion, not even the church. God is bigger than those, isn't He?

Try to explain God without using your hands, is God your hands? Try to prove the existence of God to a blind and deaf person who has never known the concept of God. Do you have to use language? Or is God just so obvious to everyone that all people for all time will be clamoring into churches that will teach them who to hate, who to fear, who is right, and who is wrong?! Finally, if God is on the church's side, then what on earth is the church so afraid of anyway? The peace and love of Jesus was extremely threatening to the people of His time. I suspect the same message is all too threatening for today's fundamentalist religions also. There is never someone so threatening as someone who loves everyone equally and who is at peace.

Religion is not evil. It is just a waste of time. A belief system is a belief system! It makes no difference in reality whether you read the words of God or say them instead.

They are merely words. Words are symbols of ideas in our heads. Ideas are not actual even though we use language to describe the actual. If that is so, is God contained by the limits of language and all its total dependency on ideas? Is God more than just a thought? Prove it. Draw a picture of God. Go on, draw me a picture of God! And do not use language! It is impossible. Any wise person can see this. Are you wise? Or do you follow religion based on empty words that have no existence in reality? God gave you a mind, so do not put yourself and your opinions into it! Keep it pure. Keep it quiet. Give the gift of peace to your mind and to the minds of others. The silent mind is the truly Religious mind. In it is a pure awareness that is aligned with God.

I say, "God does not exist and all Christians are evil." Does that upset you? Why? They are only words on this page printed with ink! Is there any truth to those words? What makes something real or true? I hope you are not going to tell me another "word" because then you are merely using language to describe ideas about your beliefs. Is language—words and sentences—real, or does it represent reality using the form of sound waves shaped according to how our mouths form the sounds?

Did you ever think about the origin of language and the origin of writing? God, as we know Him, did not always exist. By that I mean God did not exist in the form and concept that we know today, if we are talking about the origin of the concept of "God" using modern language.

Judaism adopted monotheism and Christianity also loved the idea. The concept of one god, however, has only existed in its present form for about three thousand years.

That makes it a rather "new" idea in terms of the history of the world. The Egyptians were using the concept of monotheism long before the Jews lifted the idea from them. Yet, history has shown how the Jews took delight when "their" God of monotheism killed the Egyptians in the Red Sea. Does God take sides if originally He came from the Egyptians and then turns His back on them? Is our idea of God duplicitous? How perfect can duplicity be? A God that preaches "thou shalt not kill" is going back on His own words, besides lying about loving everybody! I think these problems arise when we look at the history of the concept of monotheism and how it has changed over the ages. We like to think of God as "my God" and not "yours." We also think that "God loves ME, while He certainly does not love YOU." Such is our narcissism and selfishness. No wonder there have been wars over God.

This may come as a shock to some of you who have trouble reconciling the physical existence of God with the idea of God. So look at it this way. If you do not read the bible does God die? If you never pray will your heart stop functioning? Will your brain stop thinking? Will you be zapped by some thundercloud hovering in the skies? Where is God and what is God? Is God just a word? Is God confined to mere language? Describe God without using biblical concepts and instead use psychological ones. Impossible, right? Now describe God scientifically! It seems you can tell me what God is and what God is not. However, you are confined to using biblical language. You rely on quoting scripture. But those are mere words again. What if I am a Buddhist?

Buddhist thoughts about God are alien to the Buddhist religion. How would you go about convincing a Buddhist that "your" God is real? How would you go about convincing the Buddhist that his religion is false? Why does another "way to God" have to be wrong if it does not hurt anyone? Why do other religions have to "wrong" while yours is "right?" How do you even know what the other religion says, did you try it out for yourself? How do you know what is real and what is false—remember that you are the one who gets upset over what certain words mean, over what certain ideas cause you to think about! You are trying to take a swing at ghosts that exist only in your perception of the world. You are so caught up in reacting to everything! Why? Are you quick like the fox who is also dumb?

If anyone "proves" the validity of their religion's existence quoting scripture, then you are using circular reasoning which proves nothing. Reasoning is confined to language. Reasoning something is not the same as actually experiencing something. Reading printed words on a page that say "I am the Lord your God" is not the same as experiencing the reality of those words. Until you make contact with the actuality of the words in a scripture, until you experience the meaning behind biblical ideas, they are merely words to you. You can repeat them, but you are no better than a parrot. You can remember them, but you are no better than a computer. Applying the ideas contained in the scriptures to our life is what separates us from the parrots and the computers.

We have to put the principles of Truth into application otherwise we are NOT telling the truth. If the church is not following the principle of "judge not thou be not judged" then it is only a parrot. It is not a loving entity like Jesus. The Holy Spirit loves, it does not condemn. How can it condemn its own creation? That would be duplicitous, right? The Holy Spirit can only love. Love is all it is. In love there is no fear, no prejudice, no anger, no pressure, no effort. It is effortless and impersonal. It knows no slavery to language because it is guided by something greater than mere words. Love is Absolute.

Whether you agree or disagree with me is irrelevant because those are just your opinions about my opinions. Opinions are not reality, they are merely ideas. Ideas are only about the actual, they are not actuality. Only the actual is real. How many years has religion conditioned you into thinking that you are so good and another person is so bad, or vice versa? Did you ever meet the other and become his friend? You hate people who have never personally hurt you, talked to you, or interacted with you. Whenever you get angry you are fueled by fear. So why is all this negativity and scorn and prejudice in you? How "holy" is that? How peaceful is that? How loving is that? How religious is that? How intelligent is that?

You have to find out what is preventing you from being at peace. The clergy cannot do it for you, neither can a book or a therapist. Not even your best friend can help you. YOU have to ask serious questions if you want to be honest with yourself. Do you have the guts? I hope so. You may just continue believing in a belief system whether or not it deals with facts, whether or not it brings you peace. Most of religion is opinion. And you will say that your religion is better than my religion, right? Are you wrong and am I right? Which is it? How long does it take us to commit to the obvious—that conflict is inherent to the comparison of two things, ideas, beliefs? Comparison breeds conflict.

It is time we got over ourselves. It is time to start treating each other with real empathy, real gratefulness, real respect, real honor, trust, humility, grace, and love. Are those what your church preaches? Or does some phony preacher yell and scream about all the evil in the world without preaching about the good?

If you know who is going to hell, what are you doing to help them? Do you even want to help, like Jesus would help? It would not be wise to tell a Buddhist that God loves him because the Buddhist does not even *believe* in your God! Can biblical language's limited world view compensate for the barriers of language and belief? Why can't we show compassion for each other instead? Compassion is universal.

Why do we have to resort to finite biblical concepts that are irrelevant to today's world of electricity, cars, computers, genetic engineering, and cyberspace? Biblical knowledge is not absolute because the bible was written by men who had perceptions of reality. God did not write the bible. Men did. That is a fact that has nothing to do with opinion. Man's thought system based on fear is not Absolute. In Absolute thought there is no "other." There is no fear because there can only be One Absolute Thought which is Love. Only loving as God loves is Absolute. We need to make contact with the Absolute thought system of God which does not know fear, time, space, or comparison to *anything*. In Absolute thought there cannot be any "other" because all is One. Keep your religious language to yourself. It breeds conflict and fear. To love someone is better than to preach to them. Why? Because love is not a word but an action.

Tell me this: how is an *angry* preacher a *peaceful* preacher? How is preaching from anger more credible than speaking from peace?

Did you know that some preachers still believe in witches? Does this "belief" have any credibility or is it just another knee-jerk reaction by the church to condemn anything it does not understand or agree with? Certain "witches" were interviewed by an evening news program. In their practices they were doing nothing illegal or disrespectful to others and their property. The practices were done in private. They were not hurting others. These same witches do not consider themselves "evil." Did you know that those witches were practicing ancient healing arts and *rituals* not unlike certain church *rituals*? Why are they wrong if they are peaceful, healing, and do not harm anyone or the environment? Why are they "offensive" or "evil?" The church slaps labels on everything without ever finding out the truth behind those labels.

Some preachers believe that those "witches" are evil even though most of them use herbs and recite rituals not unlike your own religious rituals. What makes yours more or less believable or holy than theirs? Because God said so? Point to God for me. What does He say *now*? Do not point to or quote past scriptures. What does God say *today*? Is God even concerned with people who are given an arbitrary name like "witches?" Is God still up there worrying—in all His great power? I do not think so.

That may be how you see God. However, it is not the way I see God. Once again, you can tell me your opinion, and I will tell you mine. We can agree or disagree. Both mean nothing. Mere understanding or disagreeing is still at the thought level. It is still at the level of ideas. God deals with the actual, the real. God is waiting for US to get out of our heads and start living life free of prejudice, free of fear, free of dogma. God's way is the path to freedom, not your way, not my way. It cannot be found in writings, or books, or lectures, because those are still just ideas and words. To know God is to have the experience of Him yourself. Is it possible to know when you have experienced the Truth of God?

What if I cannot see God the way you do? Why is it you see your God and witches see their God? Which set of eyes is working and which set of eyes is false? Be honest with yourselves, if you even know what that means. Most of us are so numb to what is actual, we think it has something to do with personality. You say, "Oh I like him because his beliefs *feel* right to me." Is there any truth to them? Do not deceive yourself about someone's opinion being real and another opinion is false. These are serious matters because opinions rule the world.

We never question them. You do not even question your own opinions. We just go on in a state of stupor. Nothing has vitality anymore! Where are our guts?! Please hold the preacher to his words. Demand honesty from yourself and others. Why are the Egyptian Gods deemed non-existent but your God really exists? Because a book says so? How do you know the book is true? Because your God said so? When did God tell you that, at breakfast this morning?

We have to undo the illusions we live under. Illusions are regulating our lives to such a degree that we never question the validity of anything anymore. Everything is taken for granted. In doing so, the world becomes a very dangerous place with increased violence. We have lost our own voice. We have lost our own vulnerability. We have lost our innocence. The process of questioning everything, like we have done here, is necessary to break down the barriers we have constructed in front of God. This process is necessary before we can even get to "know" God beyond all our opinions and rhetoric behind relative knowledge. This breaking down of our idolized opinions is necessary before we can enter the Absolute thought system of God. This process is called disillusionment. It means, literally, to take the illusions away. It is part of the purification process. It feels bad, but that is because what we consider to be "bad" is actually a part of our comfort zone. Letting go of anything is only as difficult as we decide it to be. In reality, letting go is only a decision. We need to let go of the illusions we have made and choose a different path to God—*a path that is not of our personality, free of opinion, free of ideas, free of anything manmade.* Man did not create God. Therefore it is not wise to take anyone else's word to be "the word of God." You have to find out for yourself what God is. There is no other way.

There must be another way to discover our holiness than the way we were taught. We are so conditioned in fear. There must be another way to talk about religion without distorting the message of the Holy Spirit. There must be another way to connect with our God-nature, the Christ within. There must be another way to see the world free of illusions.

Certain people throughout history have come down to this plane of reality to teach us about God. They were able to do so without compromising there own sense of self. Each teacher of God discovered for himself what God is. Each savior belonged to no one but himself. What else is a savior but one who speaks the word of God from one's own experience, one's own inner fire? Jesus belonged to Himself. Could you say that? Each one of us has that capacity. You can do it. You can still keep your job, you can still go to church, you can stay in the same religion, you can still get married. No one is going to ask you why you were not Mother Teresa. You will only be asked why you were not yourself. Saviors are themselves… for God.

I choose to believe that it is the **content** of God's power and truth moving through us in the **form** of doing good deeds and being of service to the world. I do not believe in violence. I do not believe in hiding behind the past. I do not condone hypocrisy or enabling another person's fantasy or illusion. I do not believe in withholding love from another. I do not believe in not apologizing for wrongs done to another. All of us need to be held responsible for, and own up to, the mistakes we have made in the past. Things must come up in order to come out of our systems. That is what letting go, setting free, non-attachment, and forgiveness are all about.

In reality we have done nothing wrong because there is only life and circumstances. We project meaning and feelings onto them. That is a fact. We have merely *agreed* on a few things like "thou shalt not kill" – it seems to be a really good idea, yes? Morality is an agreement, it is not necessarily the "one right way" to live life. But morality does make life very convenient if a few ground rules are agreed upon. The universe does not need to forgive anyone because that would mean that creation has gone wrong and that life itself is some sort of biological mistake made by God. Can this be? Did God miscreate a few life forms? Some people evidently think so. However, I tend to think that those people are only misperceiving the object of their perception. That does not make the object "wrong" or a mistake on God's part.

Perhaps this is the real meaning of sin, after all. Perhaps sin is merely the archery term it actually is, which means "you missed the mark." Our misperceptions have nothing to do with seeing reality as it is. They have everything to do with seeing a lack of love. We would rather see the person in front of us as guilty, rather than a human being in need of the kind of wisdom that comes from unconditional love. Unfortunately what most of us tend to see instead of the person in front of us is a label of some abstract idea about the person without ever knowing anything beyond our own limited and ignorant opinions, prejudices, biases, knowings, and preconceived notions. This is dishonest seeing and it has ruined human relations since time began. Haven't we had enough? Haven't you ever questioned whether sin is real or if it's just some ridiculous judgment coming from a self-convinced tradition that preaches *judge not thou be not judged*? There is no such thing as sin in reality. It doesn't exist except in the minds of men, where a lot of other imaginary beasts roam also. That doesn't make them true. That doesn't mean they need to have power over us anymore. Get rid of it.

There is no lack in the universe except within our perceptions. The only lack is in our unwillingness – *not our inability* – to see beyond our projections. People are merely living their lives. Be nice to them and stop trying to control everyone else, foisting onto them your opinion of what you think their life ought to be. Is that following the Golden Rule? Well, is it??!! Have you ever realized that you just might be creating a conflict whenever you insist on defending against something? We create what we defend against.

Are you beginning to see the inherent and automatic peace that can result in releasing your fears? Do you still want to hold on to your conflicts as you compare everyone to *your* precious standards? Should we do that to you and see how you hold up? If you desire something that you are not getting (like wanting someone to change who they are just to suit *your* needs so you won't have to be so darned uncomfortable anymore) ask yourself what you are not giving to the situation. Only what we are not giving is what is lacking in any situation. Think about that before you read the next sentence. What is the point of reading anything if you're not going to be honest with yourself?

Are you always concerned with what you get from others, and from life? Or are you concerned with putting as much uplifting, nurturing, supportive, loving, compassionate and positive energy into life as you can? Why or why not? When people talk to you are you negative – constantly criticizing, condemning and complaining about how nothing is quite good enough for you? What about

YOU – are you God? Who made you the Perfection Police, anyway? Get real and be nice!

Do you complain about your problems without doing anything about them? Do you have endless hours to complain but lack all the brains to live with the wisdom to know that there are no problems apart from the mind? If you did not catch that last sentence, better stay with it until your thoughts go silent. Then there would not be any problems, there would be only peace. Get it? There are no victims in this universe. In reality there are no problems. We hardly ever know what a real need is. We think love is a Hallmark card or a fax. It isn't. So just calm down. What is the need for feeling attacked unless you are the one thinking attack thoughts in the first place? Fear is an idea that *we* made up. Let it go. Cheer up – you might die tomorrow. Who knows?

Would you rather be right or would you rather be at peace?

I am going to ask you – the reader — this question again because I am about to explain the point of this chapter to you. Would you rather be right or would you rather be at peace? Think about this. Don't read the next paragraph until you have discovered something new about yourself in light of this question. Do this now, taking as long as you need, because if you *truly* understand the power inherent in this question then this question, alone, could change your life. This one question and your response to it could be enough to enlighten you. Therefore, look at the question again and meditate on it as long as you like. It will transmit its own energy to you awakening your higher potentials. Do this now.

What do you think of this chapter? What are your opinions about it? What are your feelings, hmm? Stop right now for five minutes and think about all the thoughts, feelings, and perceptions you felt as you read this last chapter. Do this now, before reading any further, otherwise you will not experience the maximum opportunity for learning this valuable lesson. Stop for five minutes and review what your mind went through. Write it down. Then look at each item.

Finished? Now I want to tell you something. Nothing you've read in this chapter means anything. Nothing. Also, you have given everything you've read and seen all the meaning you would have it be. You chose your own reactions to the words on the page printed with ink. They are but symbols of the symbols of ideas, thoughts, and opinions. All of it is projected. All of it is composed of images that we have made.

So now ask yourself if any of the ideas I expressed were real or not. Do this now. Why did you believe them or not? Next, I want you to undo all the thoughts, feelings, and perceptions you experienced by questioning their validity *in truth*. The points of this part of the exercise are to: 1) have you experience someone else's rhetoric (or lack thereof); 2) be emotionally engaged by the opinions expressed; and then 3) step back and ask yourself if any of it is real in *truth* or are you merely caught up in reaction to something that you have projected in the first place? Did you *believe* that what I was saying was real – why or why not? Ask yourself these questions and then apply this process to the rest of your life.

Wisdom requires this kind of discrimination between what is true and what is false. It never accepts anyone else's word to be the truth because their word about your experience is literally *not your experience.*

If you survived reading this last chapter with your wits intact, your insomnia cured, or your blood pressure at normal, then congratulations! You are not easily swayed and that's one of the first steps not only to personal integrity, self-esteem, and soul empowerment, but it is also the first step towards real wisdom. It will be your wisdom and not mine, not your neighbor's, not your parents', not anyone else's but your own. This kind of personal freedom from opinions (including your own) will help you on your path of undoing all that is false because it is only a projection. Wisdom leads to inner peace and we can't have inner peace as long as we're caught up reacting to the outer world. Go within and discover your own higher intelligence that is beyond all opinions and words. Discover the space of silence and allow peace to flow there effortlessly.

This chapter was written solely to provoke you into being either curious or furious. Only we can know in any given moment the temperature of our thoughts or emotional state. This power to recognize and be self-aware is the awakening of your consciousness. We must always have an awareness of what is being said and be able to tell whether the ideas expressed are real or not. This is the correct use, the positive and creative use, of judgment. It is also called discrimination. It is our spiritual radar that tells us whether or not we are becoming more peaceful or more perturbed. Our feelings are like the emotional nervous system telling us what is going on in our heads so we can address it and *act* from there rather than *react*. How easily provoked are you? How strong is your faith and trust in yourself? How reactive are you? How volatile are you?

Look at history. Look at the past. Look how easily provoked we have been to each other! No wonder we have very little wisdom and no world peace. We need to reverse the process of projection/reaction and start being more aware and acting from that space instead. How is your self-awareness? If this chapter provoked you to feel anything other than peace, and instead got you all worked up into reaction to the point that your mind was full of thoughts and opinions rather than being silent and peaceful, then perhaps the rest of the book will help you. No matter what your reactions were, when you're done reading the whole book just start over and re-read it. The quotes I have chosen will go deeper into your consciousness and you will access deeper meanings with each new reading, until your mind comes to peace.

Remember that wisdom means that only *we* can be in charge of our emotions and perceptions no matter what anyone else says – no matter how convincing or unconvincing they are. Do not undermine yourself by allowing your experience of life to be interpreted (or misinterpreted) by anyone else only to have them hold their opinion about you to be "right" while your own views about yourself are somehow wrong. *You* be in charge, but not at the expense of harming anyone, anywhere, at any time in the universe and this includes yourself. Don't be swayed. Don't be like sheep. Find out for yourself what is preventing you from being at peace.

Discover the truth that is beyond someone else's words. Truth can only be found in silence, because silence cannot be interpreted with clumsy words. In that auspicious space, no opinions can be heard from *any* side. In the silence of peace, there is no "other" to compare to. Silence is the gateway to wisdom. Rambling, babbling, and bad writing are not silence. Truth needs no defense. The truth is defenseless, and therein lies our safety and peace. Try it. It's wonderful. Did you know that the Quakers begin each business or community meeting with silence? And they also don't end a meeting until there is a consensus – not a majority vote. Consensus lends itself to the principle of silence because in consensus there is also no "other" to compare to. Conflict ends when comparison ends. So far in this world, all we have done is compare in order to contrast. How about seeing the similarities for a change, is that so difficult? What would you rather have: conflict or peace? You decide.

Religions of the world, and people in general, have always fought over who is right and who is wrong. This chapter was an example of showing you just how easily each one of us can be swayed into reaction without first deciding whether or not something is even worth reacting to. Don't take someone else's word for granted. Do not even allow someone else to speak for your own experience because that is dishonesty. Someone else's borrowed words are not your own. This also means that we should never take anything personally when someone gives an opinion about us. Opinions are not the truth about us. They are fiction. The trap of reaction distracts us from the truth about ourselves *and* the person in front of us.

Don't get caught up in all the utterly meaningless propaganda out there. You don't need your newspapers and TVs and radios to fill the boredom in yourself. Why do you need so many other people telling you how to feel, think, or perceive? Can *you* be in charge for once? Just once? When you feel tempted to react strongly to words, next time just stop and ask yourself, "What would make me react? Why am I upset – is it for the reason I think?" Keep asking these questions as long as the answers keep coming. When you are left with the question instead of an answer and your mind is quiet, then you're almost there. Now all you have to learn how to do is sustain that inner peace for longer and longer periods. Let go of everything in your mind. Release and relax. Let go of this entire chapter. Choose peace instead.

None of us will ever learn to get along peacefully in the world until we learn to let go of the past and all of its opinions that separate all of us by a fictional account of reality. We must step out of reaction and find our own space of inner peace. Go for the action of peace, not the reactions of almighty opinions. Would you rather be right, or would you rather be at peace? You decide. It's your mind. Don't put anything false into it. Learn to appreciate a sense of wonder and amazement, mystery and uncertainty. Real wisdom is being totally at ease with complete uncertainty. Settle for nothing but the truth. Only then can it set you free.

Welcome To Peace!

We're glad you made it here.
Our number one goal
Is to Love people
so that all of us may live and love in peace.
Set both your personal and professional
goals high, as we have great confidence
in your ability to achieve them
with infinite peace and unconditional love.

<u>The Rules of Inner Peace are as follows:</u>

Rule #1: Love

There will not be additional rules.

Please feel free to ask your
Higher Self, who abides in Silence,
any question at any time.
Thank you.

Extending
Wisdom

Extending Wisdom

L IKE GOING TO A GURU, CHURCH, OR expert, this book is about listening to wisdom. Unless you apply it to your life, the message you hear in church and the wisdom you read in this book mean nothing. You have to use it to reap its rewards. I wonder if you know what I am talking about... *you* have to use it, *you* have to do it. You! God cannot save you, Buddha cannot save you, Shiva cannot save you, Holy Mother cannot save you and Jesus cannot save you unless you heed their lead. They are the examples. They have proven that a life of purity and goodness and truth can be done. *It is possible.* You cannot say that it works. You cannot say that it does not work. It is who you are, the real you, your True Self created in God's image. The "truth" is not a word. It is an action. It is literally the action of your life living itself. Life Action! Tara Singh once said, "God gave you life and you think *you* are preserving it!"

God has spoken but have we heeded?

How many people have come and told us the way of happiness? I can think of several. Did we listen? Some of us do. Do we have the capacity to recognize the truth when it is spoken? Some of us can. The truth is true no matter who says it, reads it, writes it, or speaks it. You cannot hear it or see it if you do not first discover it for yourself and listen to its song of freedom and look into the eyes of eternal joy.

What is the lifestyle of joy? It knows no fear. What is the lifestyle of love? It knows no hate. What is the lifestyle of guiltlessness? It knows no judgment. What is the lifestyle of freedom? It knows no religion in the world, only the religious mind. And religion is not a mantra or a dogma or even a belief system. The religious lifestyle is united with Truth, Love, and genuine respect toward others who are on their own Path. There are as many Paths to truth as there are people in the world. The important thing is to get there, eventually. Truth does not recognize anyone as more special than another. Truth does not hit someone over the head with dogma, reward and punishment, guilt, fear and lovelessness. For that is the dark way and it will not work anymore. We must come together as a world of people living together in peace. That is the Way, the Truth, and the Light. Or else we will not survive at all, let alone live in peace. We will only "Rest In Peace." You have to play *your* part in *your* life otherwise who will *if you do not?*

Judgment against the other has to end. There is no love in it. That is a fact. Do not attack another, you are only attacking yourself. Do not spread fear and evil. You are only walking in illusions anyway so do not make more of something that does not really exist in Truth. How foolish do you want to be?

If you are wise, you will listen to what I am saying and not judge the speaker by who says it, but listen, instead, to the Truth of it. Can you live in Truth? Can you heed the wisdom of the ages, of the gods, of your God? Can you see that all of them are saying the same thing? The point of all this is: either you are intending to love another or you are intending to attack another.

You have to choose how you will live your life. What are the principles? What are the eternal laws? Can you set aside your opinions for once and listen to the other, really listen? Put away your arrogance, it is a waste of time. Put away your fears, they mean nothing. You are nobody special, and yet you are the light of the world. It does not matter what the circumstances of your life are. Start now. You can still keep your job, you do not have to join the clergy or manifest as a nun. You can live in the world and still come into contact with the God in you, the Love in you, the Christ in you. Let the Spirit move through you, it will lift you up. It will lift away the illusions from your eyes. Living with wisdom is remembering your spirit.

If there is a God, then fine. If there is not, fine also. Either way, God can be an idea in your heart and mind. So which way do you want to go?

You have to choose. Would you rather live by the Truth of God and a lifestyle of peace? Or the idea of fear and a lifestyle of never having enough, of never finding happiness within, of never knowing Love? You choose.

Jesus cannot come down and have breakfast with you and tell you which way to go. He has already spoken. You just have to *listen* to it.

Nevermind "What would Jesus do," "What would Buddha do," "What would Machiavelli do," or even "What would Harry Potter do?"

What would YOU do?

This is where we are today. Now is the time to get over our prejudices, our anger, our fears about the "others" of the world — whether that "other" is a religion, nationality, business, or neighbor. It is time for another thought system to burst forth into our consciousness. It is time we recognize that another path is no different from our own because they all have the same Source speaking in whatever language is right for them. Get over your arrogant superiority and angry judgment of them— they are both just a lie! Let go of any narcissistic tendencies. They offer nothing of love or hope or peace. All of it is called fear, and you need to get rid of it. It is called *the history of religion* and we need to end it. Love knows no fear. Period.

Man has the will to choose a different way. Fear is by man, whereas Love is by God. You be the example of love. You be the fearless one. You be the light because that is your function here. Give your love to somebody... **anybody!** What is holding you back? You need to find out. Have some urgency! Life is a decision that **you** make. God just gave us the guidelines, the rules, and the wisdom of the ages.

Our world is caught up in an enormous cycle of action and reaction. Is there any way to step out of time into the eternal? Yes. Is there any way to step out of the realm of relative knowledge with all its likes, dislikes, wantings, opinions, jealousy, hatred, and no peace? Yes. Is there another way to see the world that is totally independent of religious dogma and ritual? Yes. What is this way?

Listen to this story of the Buddha. Someone once asked Buddha, "What is the way to God?" And Buddha replied, "Ah! There's a way!" Do you have any idea what that means? I wonder if you would take the time to figure it out for yourself. You say, "No, man! I paid for this book and I want you to tell me what it all means!" Well, I could tell you, but that would only be an idea to you. It would take you going on a journey to find out for yourself what it means.

But you would say, "Oh geez! I don't have time to do this crap! Spirituality is 'in' right now, and I just need you to give me a little bit so I can hold an intelligent conversation with my friends who are really getting into this…this GOD stuff."

Well, I could tell you what it says. It will not mean anything to you, though. It deals not with conceptual knowledge, the knowledge of the world. It deals with the absolute knowledge of the Universe. It knows no fear, it feels no hate. It does not have to judge because its light is so clear, so radiant that it casts out all darkness. We can call it "Love" but that is still just a word, a name. The Absolute cannot be contained in such small ideas and words as ours. We have very limited capacity for seeing the infinite. The Truth is not a word, as such. It is an experience.

It is not dogma or ritual either. Those are just banal activities that mankind has made trivial and meaningless. In the great scheme of things, all your rituals and little sayings will not make any difference. You have more rituals than India!

Do you think the infinite is in a ritual? Or a word? Do you even know what I am talking about? I wonder if you even want a glimpse of it for yourself. Faith is just another belief, an idea. Please be honest with yourselves. Do you ever wonder what, if anything, is real according to your religious dogmas and its prejudices? Does it merely separate your belief system from another belief system? Or does it love everybody, equally?

We are very proud of ourselves. And there is nothing more meaningless than a proud person who knows nothing about himself or his family or how to be in touch with Nature that gave him life. It is Nature that gives us life, not the government, not your phony rituals, sayings, mantras, or getting down on your knees. They give you the FEELING of accomplishment. But what has it accomplished, is it real? Or are you so caught up in the endless, boring momentum of going here, going there, without even knowing WHY you go anywhere?!

The process of getting to the truth involves disillusionment. It is necessary to bring you to a state of being disillusioned, so that all your illusions are taken away. At least you can be honest with yourself and say that you know what you are doing and why! When you are coming from that space within of having something to give, rather to want, then you are free.

But most of us are so caught up in our belief systems, our prejudices, that we do not know what is real and what is just the thinking of the brain! You are very clever, you know. The brain can do anything, manufacturing all kinds of wild religious stories. Are they real? We can never "know" the present because we immediately make it thought; an idea. If your mind turns to words, you are not in the present dealing with the actual. Reality is not a word.

Only the actual is real. What is real in your life that is free from opinion? Anything? Your opinions change, they are not timeless. Probably they are not even yours to own, hmm? Do you say anything real? Have you made contact with the infinite inside? I hope you will see that I am not just babbling. I am asking questions so that you will open your eyes and step out of your crazy momentum for just a while. Maybe in that state of waking up, you will get to know yourself for the very first time. Maybe you do not even KNOW who you are or what your function is here on earth. What is your purpose? Is it your job? Is it to please your boss? Is it to wait for the stock options? Is it living paycheck to paycheck, is it merely plodding along one day at a time, squelching the joy out of you, ignoring all the questions, deadening the pain of existence, just living a dead life?

A lot of us take a little drink, some alcohol, some drugs, some sexual affair to deaden the pain. They bring us down to sub-level so we are not feeling the actual anymore. We are no longer in contact with what is real. So we dull ourselves! What sense is that? It smacks of fear. We are all full of fear, but there is a way out. Disillusion is a means of freeing ourselves from the mundane, the hateful, the angry, and the depressing sides of life.

It is the gate we must walk through in order to see clearly. If you want it badly enough, you will do it for yourself. Never take another's word for it—it may be their truth in actuality, but to you it is just an idea. You have not experienced it for yourself so do not BEGIN to judge or criticize it. Your judgments and criticisms will not mean a thing. They would be meaningless. Until you find out the Truth for yourself, you will not have confidence in yourself, you will not "feel loved" by the world. You will be in a constant state of attack, perceiving attack from all sides. Therefore you attack back. If you perceive a lack of love in the world, a lack of ANYTHING, then that is the very thing you are not giving to the world.

When you realize the Truth about who you are and why you came here, all of this will seem very simple. Until then it will seem crazy. It does not matter if you understand it or not. It does not even matter if you LIKE it or not— you have to live your life in actuality or you are living a dead life. When will you start to undo the illusions? The only responsibility we have is to ourselves. When we love ourselves, then we love others. When you have something to give rather than to want, you are home. There is no greater joy than helping someone in need. That is called "EXTENDING" the wisdom of love. It is a light so bright, that the more you give, the more you have.

It is the Law of the Universe and it is totally independent of dogma. It is beyond religion because it does not deal with the petty ideas of separation that have ruled this world for thousands of years! All your so-called "religion" promotes ideas like "this people is chosen" and "this people is not good enough" and "this people must be killed" and "this people must be hated because the word was not spoken to them" and so on and so on. Is there any Truth to it? Is there any love for the other person in it? Unless it is love for *everybody* then it is not love. It is only your preference or your prejudice. Which will you choose: a religion based on outdated, centuries-old dogma that makes no sense in a modern world...or peace?

Is any judgment based on actuality and love? No. All of it is based on fear. It is the human condition to fear that which we do not understand or cannot control. And because we cannot seem to control each other, (let alone ourselves!) then we manufacture intricate ways of misperceiving the person in front of us. We have constructed very clever ways to separate ourselves from reality and the love inherent within it. We have built entire nations founded on belief systems based on fear, hate, and reward and punishment. What is the sense of loving one person and not another? You really begin to question the motivations of everything. Hold the preacher to his words! Put people on the spot—are they speaking from actual experience? Did Jesus have breakfast with them and chat about all this? YOU find out. You have to do it or no one else will. The therapist cannot open your eyes. You have to be willing to undo the illusions. Why? Because you can and you will, sooner or later. Why wait? "There's no time like the present!"

Questioning starts the Path by undoing. When you question life, you start the awakening process. You accept nothing as it is. You will begin to question the motivations, the ambitions, the hidden fears. You may think that all this is a waste of time. But I assure you that NOT doing it is not only a waste of your time but a waste of your life. You probably have never made contact with the infinite within yourself! If you did, it would not be lost, it would not run out, you would not feel deprived, lost, or unhappy.

When you discover for yourself what your function is then no preacher, no guru, no therapist can take it away from you, or increase it either. Love is the ultimate gift from God to His son. It is in YOU. Start now. You do not need someone else to awaken you, you can do it for yourself. Once you are awakened, you are free.

Do you want to be free of sadness, anger, and confusion? You would probably say: "No—I need insecurity; I need activity; I need my prejudices; I need to be totally dependent upon someone else for my happiness; I am still waiting for someone to tell me she loves me and I cannot be at peace until she tells me; I cannot forgive anyone because I am angry and I do not want to change because I am too old to change… leave me alone with my problems!" Okay, we will! How monotonous. How boring. No wonder no one wants to talk to you— you disgust people with all your ungratefulness! Can you see how all that negativity is not very *attractive*? In other words, you are not literally attracting love in your life because of all your misperceptions of fear.

You will begin to see how the monotony of certain activities (like complaining about what you lack) is just taking up valuable time, "killing time," and killing your peace of mind—not to mention the peace of mind of anyone weak enough to allow you to go on and on. What would a *real friend* do, let you remain in your illusions or try to wake you up? The most loving person would be bold enough to put you on the spot! He would not settle for anything less than *your* peace of mind—even if that means telling you something you do not like to hear…it just might be the Truth about you. Look in the mirror, folks!

But you do not want to wake up, you have never *been* awake! If you were held accountable for *all* your actions and words, you would be horrified by all your insecurities, unhappiness, hidden anger and hate. Most of what you call love is actually hate—you "hate" to hear the truth, right? The wise person would show interest in hearing what someone else has to say. The wise person *loves* to hear the truth about himself. Only the fearful ones take umbrage when the truth is told about them. They cower in more and more fear until one day all hell breaks loose and they have a heart attack. Whoever still believes the mind-body connection is not real is still living in the dark ages, and I am surprised they are not more depressed than they already are.

The most loving person would probably offend you because that person would not accept your misery and petty "needs" based on your perception of a lack of love in your life. You have designed needless activities to cure the boredom within yourself. You have built enormous resistance to *listening* to people when they communicate their feelings to you. You are not at peace if you cannot handle honest feelings coming from someone else. Do you have the greatness of Jesus to merely listen without perceiving attack? No…you will defend yourself, and then run for your life—if you live that long! Sooner or later life gets in your face and it WILL wake you up, *whether you want to wake up or not.* That is called the course of your life, which is a course in miracles. Are you aware of all the miracles around you or do you still hate your life and some people in it? If you have any fear at all, or any anger, you are not perceiving correctly, you are not thinking at all, and most importantly you are not at peace. Are you going to find out what is preventing peace now? Still not convinced that there are no problems in life? Okay…keep reading.

You could be helping someone else instead of listening to some stupid speech or lecture on how guilty you are. There is enough fear in the world, so when will you question its authenticity? *When will you wake up?!* Tell me—when will you be free?! Only love is real. Fear is false. You are making it up.

You will not be free if you are satisfied with anything other than peace. You are quite satisfied with your misery and pain, you just go on and on. You claim you are not feeling loved, you say that someone never loved you the way you wanted to be loved—which is still the greedy mentality of "getting." You are still thinking: "What am I going to *get* from life?" rather than the healthy perspective that asks: "What can I *give*, rather than *get*?" You are still misperceiving the world through the eyes of lack. You cannot sit back and claim that the world or a person owes you something whether it is more money, more love, or a Hallmark card. Forget about them and give *yourself* peace! Can you do that? How arrogant are you to think you do not deserve peace? Living **without** anger, stress, and delusions of misperceived lack *is humble*—not arrogant. Are you at peace and is all the anger and rage gone now? Are you convinced yet that YOU have to undo your fears? No one else can give you peace—that is a deception. Only YOU are preventing peace, no one else. Stop blaming the world, stop blaming your family, stop blaming your relatives, stop blaming your friends. Stop blaming the devil, or God. *YOU* are the problem, so *YOU* fix it.

If people have expressed their feelings to you about something you did that hurt them in the past, have *you* asked for their forgiveness? Did you take the higher road? Or did you just play the pathetic game of crucifixion, denying everything they said and then shut them out of your life? If someone has something to say to you, then do you have the space within to listen to it? Is there enough love in your heart to hear the other person's feelings—no matter what they are? Probably not. Only you know. You are in charge of your happiness…or misery.

You are not healed and you are not at peace if you believe you were cheated out of something. But what do you ever DO about it? Are you transformed? Do you merely bitch about life because bitching gets you attention and sympathy from others who are too weak to take a stand with you and not allow you to perpetuate your false insecurities and problems? There is no need for you to play so low any more. There is no need for you to be unhappy anymore. It is unnecessary for you to "need" attention from others so much that your feelings are hurt if you do not hear from them. Where is your voice of sacredness? The only appropriate way to extend wisdom is to love the person in front of you—*unconditionally*. If you love with *your* conditions then you will feel as if the other person is loving YOU with *their* conditions.

In other words, you will feel as if the other person is withholding love even though you have probably been dishing out crap by withholding love *yourself.* Where is your faith now, sir? Do you have faith in peace or do you have faith in separation from peace? Is your mind silent as you read these words? Be honest.

There is no such thing as a faithless person. You either have faith in love, or faith in fear. But you consider someone who expressed his feelings to you, or asked you pointed questions that would lead you to undo all your illusions, to be the "bad guy." Are ever grateful for such communication? You are still full of denial and hate. Do you like what is told to you or do you hate it? I would relish the opportunity for someone to tell me the truth. Someone expressing her feelings is a *treasure, a gift,* not an evil act. We are released by truth, not more enslaved by it. Will you be released—or will you dig your heels in, continue cowering behind your walls of denial, and blame the other for attempting to help you get free?

This reminds me of what people probably said about Jesus who did a lot of His healing simply by telling the truth. He pointed out facts and spoke up about specific behaviors people were performing that needed to be changed. Imagine people saying this about Jesus: "Oh, I think there must still be a lot of anger in you to bring up all this negativity in people!" Hardly. Now THAT is laughable! Could you hear the truth if Jesus spoke it to you? Would you deny what He would say?

Would you even recognize the truth if it were told

to you? Probably not! You would merely get upset, throw a temper tantrum and pout like a small child who just got scolded. See how ungrateful we can be? See how we lack the discrimination to see the truth that can set us free? We dislike hearing the truth because the mind has tremendous resistance to it. That resistance is called *the dark way*. The dark way masquerades itself, rallying for sympathy by claiming a lack of love. Followers of the dark way take umbrage for having the mirror of truth held up to their face—the mirror that says, "This is who you are, this is your behavior, and you need to stop it." Most people cannot handle that much light.

It tends to blind them and they run off into darker catacombs where blame, fear, anger, and denial seethe in the night. The wise person welcomes the truth. The wise person can handle the truth. The wise person denies what is of fear, not allowing it to run its course. Are you such a person? If you are not at peace with *everyone* then you are not wise because somewhere you still have fear or a sense of being attacked. Let it go. Choose again. Have more faith in the process of atonement than you do now.

The only appropriate extension of wisdom is the love you give to another—not the love you want to *get*. Loving another means you will not let them live their life in fearful illusions. If you are enabling a brother by letting him continue to perceive incorrectly, then you are not at peace either and YOU need to wake up! If you were wise, this fact would be obvious, it would be a clarity of pure thought. The light of truth is obvious for those who see it. If you get upset when someone tells you something, you are hiding from something. If you deny that person the space to communicate their honest feelings to you, then you are violating something. Truth is helpful to (and *welcomed* by) those who have the eyes to see and the ears to hear.

If you lack the love to help another, you cannot extend wisdom. Extending the truth is an act of gentleness. Find out what is preventing you from extending gentleness. How about YOU be the one to stop complaining, stop whining about your life and get on with loving others instead, huh? Is that so bad? Is that so difficult? People might actually LIKE you more if you were more pleasant to be around and listen to. You can afford to be more interesting than just being someone who hates life but does nothing about it. It reminds me of the saying: If you are bored, you will bore someone else also!

It does not have to be this way. It is time we get a hold of ourselves and really delve into what religion is supposed to be about. Is it about fear? Or is it about love? The love is within YOU. No one can take it away, but you have to awaken it first. Afterwards, you will know no greater happiness, no greater peace, no greater love than to extend it to everything and everyone in sight. Love does not judge. Love gives. Love does not know fear or hate. Love just is. Love does not know "us versus them" and exclusivity. Love is INCLUSIVE. Love does not know "my religion is absolutely right and yours (if you even have one) is absolutely wrong." Love does not judge! Love is not anger, or control masked as charismatic leadership. Love is gentle, even when it speaks loudly at times, because love is gentle, fear is not.

Listen to the song of silence, it is the music of life—

a melody that is your own. Have you ever heard the song of happiness? Why not?! Are you convinced yet— that peace is not only desirable, but urgently needed? If you are wise, your opinions would be silent now.

At the end of this book you will find various quotes about extending wisdom and love. If the meaning is not readily apparent perhaps you need to awaken first, or maybe spend a little more time seeing beyond the mere words which are only symbols of symbols. Find out the actuality of them, not just the intellectual ideas *about them.* The truth will awaken you. The scriptures *can awaken you if you have the attention.* They will awaken within you a greater capacity for love. There is no such thing as a "love overdose" so don't worry—you cannot have too much of it. There is nothing better to do than to really get to know YOURSELF. Never undermine yourself. Never undermine another human being. It is a waste of time. Love them instead, if you have it to give. If you do not, WHY NOT? Go and find out. That IS your function. When you discover that, you will no longer have to worry about how to live or which way to live or what to believe....you ARE living and you ARE loving!

The only appropriate way to share love with someone, or to love someone as Jesus would do, is to show compassion for people's mistakes—*not to punish them for them; isn't there enough pain and suffering in the world without contributing MORE of that same evil stuff to it?!!* You cannot be religious is you perceive "sin" in another. You *must* love them. Do you have faith in people's potential for evil or do you have faith in people's potential for joy, love, peace, and happiness? Whomever you meet, that person in front of you is the person to whom you are supposed to be nice. *That person* was sent to you *by God* so you could prove *to God* that you know how to show love and put forth more peace into the world instead of more pain, prejudice, and suffering. If you withhold love from ANY-ONE, you are by definition choosing salvation *in separation* from God, which is still *the dark way.* That is why you cannot hate ANYONE and say that you are loving. Love is all-encompassing, and therefore is Absolute—being from God. That which is all-encompassing can have no opposite. That means that if you are to be "convicted" as a Christian, or "convicted" as being religious, you must love everybody equally—*no exceptions.* You cannot condemn others for their mistakes and call that love. That is what a lot of what religion calls love, but it is actually hate. And we all know, deep down, that there is a fine line between bitching and being downright evil. Choose peace instead.

You are the light of the world. You are nothing less than a blessed creation of the universe. Never undermine yourself nor anyone else. To put down the Son of God is blasphemous. Watch out for your ego's arrogance – it can be very clever, especially under the guise of appearing to be spiritual. True spirituality is to live as Spirit – the spirit of love and wisdom. You can be in the world and not be of the world. Find out what the difference is. Allow peace to flow effortlessly into your heart as your silent mind blesses the world. You'll find that even the stars in the sky will bow down before you. Let the heavens open up in *your* heart and then extend it to the person in front of you and then to the world. That is our function. Thank you, and God bless you.

Mencius said, "A gentleman steeps himself in the Way because he wishes to find it in himself."

Confucius

~

What thing I am I do not know. I wander secluded, burdened by my mind. When the Firstborn of Truth has come to me I receive a share in that selfsame world.

Hinduism, Rg Veda 1.164.37

~

The end and aim of wisdom is repentance and good deeds.

Judaism, Talmud, Berakot 17

~

Does not wisdom call, does not understanding raise her voice? On the heights beside the way, in the paths she takes her stand; beside the gates in front of the town, at the entrance of the portals she cries aloud; "To you, O men, I call, and my cry is to the sons of men. O simple ones learn prudence; O foolish men pay attention. Hear, for I will speak noble things, and from my lips will come what is right; for my mouth will utter truth; wickedness is an abomination to my lips. All the words of my mouth are righteous; there is nothing twisted or crooked in them. They are all straight to him who understands and right to those who find knowledge. Take my instruction instead of silver, and knowledge rather than choice gold; for wisdom is better than jewels, and all that you may desire cannot compare with her.

Judaism and Christianity
Proverbs 8.1-11

~

*If any of you lacks wisdom, let him ask God
who gives to all men generously and without
reproaching, and it will be given him.*

*Christianity
James 1.5*

~

*There is no greater wealth than wisdom;
no greater poverty than ignorance;
no greater heritage than culture.*

*Islam
Nahjul Balagha, Saying 52*

~

*True learning induces in the mind
service of mankind.*

Sikhism, Adi Granth, Asa, M.1, pg. 356

~

*This is true knowledge: to seek the Self
as the end of wisdom always.
To seek anything else is ignorance.*

Hinduism, Bhagavad Gita 13.11

~

*Whoever goes after unreasonable
and unnecessary rationalization will
never be able to reach truth.*

Islam, Nahjul Balagha, Saying 30

~

*True words are not fine-sounding;
Fine-sounding words are not true.
The good man does not prove by argument;
And he who proves by argument is not good.
True wisdom is different from much learning;
Much learning means little wisdom.*

Taoism, Tao Te Ching 81

~

On Thee alone we ever meditate,
And ponder over the teachings of the loving
mind. As well as the acts of the holy men,
Whose souls accord most perfectly with truth.

Zoroastrianism, Avesta, Yasna 34.2

~

The price of wisdom is above rubies.

Christianity, Job 28:18

~

Life is a festival only to the wise.

Emerson

~

Youth is the time to study wisdom; old age is
the time to practice it.

Rousseau

~

There Must Be a Different Way

There Must Be a
Different Way

A LL OF US CAN CHOOSE A DIFFERENT way. Each one of us has the capacity to take our place among the saviors of the world. We can continue in a direction of loving each other or we can continue to point out all the differences that separate us. Which way are you going to choose: 1) the way of always seeing humanity in separate parts, each one needing to be attacked and therefore taken under control, or 2) the way of not excluding anybody from love, the way of total peace, the way devoid of fear?

When we conclude something, we think we "know" something. In doing so, we never get to know the truth of anything. We only know "my opinion." If you make the decision to undo illusions within you, something will take place, some kind of transformation will occur within you. You will be taking one step closer to realizing the Truth of

God. You will awaken from a sleep of forgetfulness. Most of us have forgotten who we really are, and we are all holy children of God.

Our thoughts represent the voice of the ego. Service represents the voice of God. Service is the state of being in peace that allows us to give and receive love. If you understand what I am saying, mere understanding doesn't really free you. You are only agreeing with me. That is another deception of the mind. Choose again.

You have to discover the truth for yourself. Don't take my word for it. Somewhere you begin to realize that it is extremely difficult to change. Just think about trying to change your spending habits. Are you addicted to shopping and "getting" things? I don't think Jesus had a bank account. He'd have a tough time getting a home equity loan.

Heaven and hell are not places we go after we die. They also exist right here, right now. They are states of being. Hell means you are isolated. Hell is being cut off from the Truth. Hell is seeing illusions. Heaven is a state of being at peace with oneself and the world. In heaven, nothing can disturb you, nothing can deceive you. In heaven all is love, all is eternal. Heaven is in the present moment that is alive with the vitality of pure awareness. Heaven is in the present. Hell is projected from the past. Conflict is hell. Having fear is living in hell.

Heaven and hell are not the same as reward and punishment. Heaven needs no reward, as if something greater than heaven could be rewarded. Hell is not a punishment because hell is merely seeing illusions which are not real. Therefore, something that is not real cannot be punished. Heaven is real because it deals with God's unconditional love. Hell is not real but merely a state in which we have not chosen God—that is why it "feels like hell." Anything that separates us from God is like being in hell. Anything you could offer another person other than love is offering them "hell."

A state of heaven is an action that has no reaction in it. It does not need to react to anything because it has everything—it is heaven! Are you in heaven? Being in hell reacts to everything because it is the state of a lack of love, which is not of God. Succinctly, heaven is recognizing that everyone is an innocent child of God, and hell is noticing anything other than the innocence in another. Humans make mistakes, but that does not make us mistaken beings. We are all on a path to God, so can we help each other through love rather than kicking each other down with judgment? There is no greater reward than love and no greater punishment than a lack of it. Heaven deals with love only. There is no "other," like "punishment," because that would split heaven into duality. God is One. He is not split between reward *and* punishment.

Reward *and* punishment have ruled the world for thousands of years. It is a church concept. We are trained to "believe." This fills the mind with ideas. We are conditioned to believe we are helpless and in desperate need of help. We are not trained to be aware. Awareness empties the mind of thought, undoes illusions, and sees the world through the eyes of innocence. Do you have the attention to be aware?

We are taught how to fear people by seeing them as separate from us, separate from peace, separate from God.

Then we learn how to project our fears onto another. You know you are undermining yourself when you dislike somebody else because you cannot escape judging yourself if you judge somebody else. When you do that, you feel guilty. How will we ever see the innocence in another if we are always afraid of him?

The problem is not that we hate each other. The problem is that we do not *love* each other. You cannot "reward" only to have punishment waiting in the wings. Then your so-called reward is not Absolute, but shifting, changing, and always reacting. Your "reward" is part of the changing realm of knowledge called relative knowledge. The whole world is built on this kind of knowledge. Nothing in the world is Absolute. Only God is Absolute, like perfect love.

Absolute Love is part of changeless knowledge, it is pure action without reaction. Love is from God, therefore Love is eternal, never changing its *content* although its *form* might change. God is concerned with content while we are concerned with form. Had you noticed? We do not like the ways things look, or feel, or sound, or behave.

Our preferences are always changing and that is why we "feel" so guilty. That is why we "feel" like we are getting nowhere. That is why we "feel" like life has no meaning. Life has all the meaning you want to give it, but if you are coming from *form*, then the world will always seem to move away from you. When you come from a deeper place, like contentment, then the world has many forms but love is always there; you will never perceive a lack.

Life is always there to take care of you. If you completely let go of everything, life does take care of you. But you have to *completely let go*. It will seem very scary to do so, and you will want to run for your life! If you have the determination within YOU, you can do it. Jesus did it. Mother Teresa did it. Life takes care of us, not the government. This is called Life Action. It is Absolute. The action of life can help us *if we are aware*. We need nothing else. We need no one else to help us. We need only to open our own eyes and see life as it is— without projections, without illusions.

The clergy says, "Ask Jesus." Have you talked with Jesus? Do you know him personally? These are just phrases— words that sound nice. They have no meaning at all. Your brain is very clever and can make up all kinds of fantasies, dreams, aspirations, and ambitions. They are just more projections that feel comforting. Are they real, though? Are feelings, like preferences, Absolute? No. Only the Truth is Absolute. The way of Jesus is Absolute.

The Truth is very austere. The energy of Truth does not seek answers, it undoes illusions that say there are problems. In reality there are no problems. Truth is a purer energy. So we can either be the saviors of the world living in Truth, or we can manufacture more bombs and be the destroyers of peace and Love. Which way are you going to choose? The way of Truth demands determination. It is not the easy way. Hell is the easy way. Heaven takes no effort, though, because it is only a decision away. Change your mind and see a different way to live your life. Are you going to do it? No one else can do it for you. You have to live *your* life. It is possible.

The mind that sees possibilities is the mind that questions everything. This is the wise mind. The wise mind is aware, being innocent of illusions. Can we choose to be innocent or vulnerable? Vulnerability means we are defenseless and not afraid. We are so insecure and afraid because of our conditioning. In exchange for our innocence we have become defensive. This is a waste of our energy. Allow the vitalizing energy of life and peace to flow through you. Be vulnerable. Vulnerability means defenselessness.

You say, "But the world would manipulate me!" Well then let it! If you have the peace within, then what do you care? Then you start to panic, saying, "I'll lose my job!" Then lose your job! If you are reading this right now, chances are that you are not working anyway. Are you dead if you are not constantly working at your job? Of course not! You have something else in you that says you are not a victim of the external world of circumstances.

In Truth you are not a victim at all. Nothing external could affect you if you had the determination to be free. You could see past the illusions of ambition, money, fame, loss, greed, loneliness, and poverty. You would not accept anything the ego tells you. You would have found the light within yourself where there are no such things as problems. Nothing external could disturb the peace within. When you are at peace, your thoughts are born from a purer energy that is never wasteful. It only energizes you, it lifts you up. At that point you are one with Spirit.

This energy of pure thought is miraculous. It is direct from God—it is not something you "know." If it can be "known" then it is an idea and not actuality. If you are aware then you are in direct contact with God. Awareness is not a state of "knowing." Instead it is "watching." Be a witness and watch God's creation unfold. If you do this, all wanting, insecurities, and fear will be gone. It takes no effort on your part, only letting go of all effort. God will do the rest. God is in charge of the "doing" and it is up to us to relax into that.

This does not mean that you become lazy. On the contrary, you would be quite productive because your eyes would be open to all the misery and suffering in the world. Your true Productivity would offer peace instead. Do you have the eyes to see all the work you could be doing in the world instead of your own selfish, self-centered job in which you are probably enslaved by some "other authority," or some "boss" other than yourself? Are you your own boss, or do you bow down to somebody else? Why are you not in charge of your own life?! You need to find out. The saints worked for God, so who do you work for, hmm? You do not have to change jobs or quit your current job in order to do God's work. Start where you are. See the fact as a fact and do not distress over your situation. When you give your job honesty, you can do no greater work. How do you like that! What a relief, huh? Working for God is easy because the whole Universe is on your side. Try perceiving your job like this: you have a part to play in the salvation of the planet, therefore there is no greater service than to serve the world with all the love you can possibly give.

We think our "doing self-improvement" or "being spiritual" prevents us from harm. Mere "doing" or getting caught up in an activity that *feels* spiritual does not prevent anything because our "doing" is usually a *reaction* to something that we have projected. Only when we are aware do our reactions cease. We would not get caught up in the endless momentum of fearful or ambitious re-actions. Rather, we would become witnesses to the action of life.

There is no reason to be afraid anymore. You have stars guiding you. Nothing can harm you. You are the light of the world! Are you going to be grateful for that? Right now—are you grateful? *Do not allow one single negative thought to come into your brain.* Silence the monkey on your back! *You* be in charge. When questioning illusions you maintain your sacredness, accepting *nothing* from the voice of doom and the veil of fear. Discover your own in-tegrity. Have guts and determination! Make the decision *not* to be ruled by anything external.

Even **that** means you will not accept *anything I say in this book.* Instead, you would discover the truth of it for yourself. If you are *interested* in what God has provided for you in life, that interest would lead you to grateful-ness. Taking interest is the same as questioning and un-doing of thought. It is like doubt, which also questions. In the space of peace— of being aware of what is already provided— there is no fear. Isn't that beautiful? Did you even hear that? Are you grateful for your life now?!

Silence that brain of yours, it wants to have an opin-ion! It wants to be right and prove me wrong—anything but peace. See how clever the brain is? It says, "Hi, I'm your wonderfully brilliant brain and together you and I can outwit *anybody.* Together, you and I can beat anybody's logic, opinion, reasoning, *anything*!!" Ah! But will your brain be quiet? No. The brain can justify anything, includ-ing watching over itself in the name of "being spiritual."

The brain is noisy. It cannot rest. Thought will not let it. That is why YOU cannot undo thought using thought! The process of undoing thought is involuntary, impersonal, and has no motives. If you *want* to be silent, then that is not silence! Be aware. Watch. Look at the world but do not react to it. When your thoughts have stilled and the brain is resting, pure thoughts come that are objective. This voice of clarity will tell you what to do *immediately*, without hesitation, because then you would be letting *intelligence* flow through you. Intelligence is not a word. It is a pure clarity of vision. It is how God sees, being Absolute Vision.

We do not know the potential of the kind of space that is not contaminated by fear and lack of love. Can we enter the kingdom of the present and overcome our unwillingness to change? Can we be totally free from fear and align ourselves with the Peace of God?

There is no reason to wait any longer for peace. There is no more time, **any longer**, to put off peace. In fact, in a state of peace there is no time. Time does not exist anyway. It is only a collective agreement made by man to "clock," or measure, the movement of the earth around the sun. In reality there is only eternity. We need to make contact with the eternal. When time stops and you are still, that stillness is bigger than the planet. Everything we do disturbs the stillness. We get busy surviving. We get into ruts. We get into reaction. We are distracted by feelings like: "I like you," or "I think I love you— (that is, if you do only what I tell you to do!)."

If you were a real apprentice to the Truth you would put everything on the spot and question it. All our manmade problems have nothing to do with the God-created world. There is the God-created world and the manmade world that your perception has entirely made up. You only need to be in the present. The present does not shift to the past. It does not project a future. You need nothing else but the awareness of the present moment. The present is the only reality there is. Heaven is in the present! Healing is in the present! Peace is being in the present! Are you going to be in the present, now? C'mon…tell me.

Now that you understand that, you are going to make it an idea. Do not deceive yourself! Find out for yourself beyond these words, beyond these ideas, beyond this book, what it means to be in the present. Your understandings are merely misunderstandings. You have acquired more knowledge and a lot of learning but they mean nothing if YOU have not made contact with the *meaning behind the words*. The present is not a word. Find out what it is. If scriptures are true, have you made contact with their truth that is beyond *all opinion*? Ah! See how this works? Scriptures are real in the sense that they *point toward* reality. They are like the recipe, the directions, the guidelines, the instructions on how to bake the cake. But even you know that the recipe on the little card is not the chocolate cake, right? Are you beginning to see now? Undo your understandings. They are false.

What I am talking about combines all religion, and yet is no "religion" at the same time. In the present you can discover that you are a Spirit. Being in the present changes how we identify with ourselves. We usually identify with the body without extending the Spirit. When you extend from your Spirit you extend the Truth. The Truth offers miracles, clarity, holiness, everything you need in order to be in line with the universe and your own, true identity. You will be aligned with the thought system of God, which is Awareness of peace, love, sanity, gentleness, and gratefulness.

The present is untouched by time. It offers all the wisdom of the ages. In the present is everything. The tree grows in the present not in the past. We are always finding ways to escape the present through ways of self-improvement. Anything... but the present. Anything but stillness. Why? Where's that monkey now? Still there?

The energy of the present is being decimated by our thinking processes. We have to silence the brain and our thoughts because they are conditioned and programmed. Our brains are no longer our own. Our belief systems are in charge. We are enslaved by our belief systems. We never really stop to think about turning the other cheek. Is it even possible? Is there anyone alive today who has the guts and integrity to make a difference? If this country could produce one such person, that person could change the world. The present is not affected by the illusions of time, and space. The present is not affected by circumstances because the present *just is.*

We have become too dependent on the clergy's words. We can no longer hear what they are really saying. We can no longer see the light because we choose to stay in the dark. We do not have the ears to hear the Word. We do no have the eyes to see the innocence in another. Why? All our preoccupations get in the way. Do not let them. Do you ever wonder if you could be a saint? Is that just your projected ambition? If you have peace, there is no greater way for a saint to live. In peace, you are never offended, and *you offend no one.*

A lot of clergy have fanaticism, but lack the present. Look at all the people they have persecuted. "Thou shalt not kill" has killed more people (burned at the stake in the name of God) than any other. These clergy are the false prophets of God. If they cannot offer peace, if they cannot live without anger or fear, ambition, or prejudice, then they are false. Do not follow anyone false; instead follow God, and His voice of joy. Listen to Jesus. Can you forgive as He did?

Do not follow anything false. It is a waste of energy. Do not undermine yourself. The world needs you. Take good care of yourself, your family, and your children. Do you take good care of your body? I am not talking about dressing it with the latest fashions, either. Are you healthy? What is preventing your being healthy? Is anything more important than taking care of your own life? Life is a gift from God—don't mess it up. Life is sacred. *All life is sacred. Never undermine someone else's life or their experience of it. That is not your function here. Your function is to love, only.*

Take care of yourself and others. Treat your body like a temple, for it is the Spirit's home. Spirit does not need the body, but the body does need the Spirit. As long as we are alive on earth, the Spirit can love others only by communicating through the body. In reality you are not a body but a spirit communicating through a body.

Are you identified with your body? We identify too much with our bodies which leads to ultimate disappointment because the body dies. The Spirit never dies. Look at how we torture people's minds and bodies to get them to convert to other belief systems. Is one belief system better than another belief system? A belief system is a belief system! They are just opinions, there is no truth in them whatsoever. The Spirit resides in Truth, not opinions. Are you willing to make contact with the Spirit in you? Do you have the determination or is there something better to do? You decide. Use your will. Decide again.

If you had interest in determination, you could turn your life around RIGHT NOW and declare yourself FREE! Will you remain hopelessly dependent—wanting to continue reading this because you believe it will help you? If you are looking for answers then you are not at peace either. The mind that questions settles for no answers and no conclusions. When we conclude, we have lost the space to be aware. The "conclusion" fills it up because now we think we "know" something. In reality you are merely having an idea, a thought. You are not open to possibilities devoid of opinion and comparison. When we "know" we are unwittingly making ourselves unwilling to see things differently. This makes up our unwillingness. The wise person is free of conclusions, so we have to undo our unwillingness to be free.

Can we all see how each of us has unwillingness? It is so. It is very difficult to deal with. Krishnamurti once said, "People seldom ever change." Therefore, let us deal with one point at a time and see the obstacles that get in the way. I am talking about the principles of the Truth. "Truth" is not Christian, yet Christians can live in Truth. "Truth" is not Buddhist, yet Buddhists can live in Truth.

The Truth is not a word. It is a state of being. It is a lifestyle. I wonder if anybody has ever put their attention into something like discovering what the Truth actually is? Would **you** do it? Don't conclude now, be open and just wonder for a moment: "What is the Truth?" Let your mind drift, allowing it to relax with the question. Do not accept any answers to it, though. Let everything flow through you, including your judgment of these words. Let it go.

It takes a great deal of attention to have an awareness of the Truth. We have no idea what attention is. In attention there is no deception. No thought touches it. Otherwise it is not attention. We have the potential to be aware, but awareness can only come to light when we are in the present. Can you imagine that we are never in the present? Thought will not let us! Now don't get too upset by this because that would only be a fearful reaction to an idea. So just calm down. There is another way to deal with this. It is possible to learn through joy instead of pain. God would rather we learn life's lessons through joy, anyway. Happiness saves time and peace saves lives.

What, then, prevents us from having attention? Your thinking. The activity of the brain. Our good ol' friend known as "thought," and a new friend known as "personality." Your personality is only what you think the world would have you be. It is just another projection of your desire to be something else for somebody else. You want to be liked. Anything "personal" implies separation from everyone else and separation from God. Therefore nothing is *really* "personal" because all is One, in Truth. If you want to be liked then you have a belief that you are separate from everyone else. This is a deception. The fact that you are alive means not only that you are liked, but that *you are loved.* This is called the action of the present. The present loves everybody. Are you going to experience the present? Are you ever in the present?

The action of the present is impersonal. So over a million years we have been taught that the prophets would solve our problems, the clergy would lead us to truth, the guru would bring us peace—albeit in a mystical (but very cool) way. However, each one of us can step out of time, and into the present *on our own.* That is the greatest gift of God to man: our will to choose. *You* choose another way by choosing the present.

All the great religious minds of history have proven that this can be done. IT CAN BE DONE! It can be done by yourself *without the help of anyone else.* Instead of worshipping the peace in another, find it within yourself. *It can be done!* People throughout the ages have proven that it can be done.

Jesus proved it can be done—He was an example. There are, and have been, many examples of people who have done it. Do you have the eyes to see them? Look at the lives of Buddha, Lao Tzu, Confucius, Muhammad, Krishnamurti, Helen Schucman, Tara Singh, Mother Meera, Paramahansa Yogananda, Mother Teresa, Gandhi, Ramana Maharshi, Pema Chodron, The Dalai Lama, Thich Nhat Hanh, Rabbi Joseph B. Soloveitchik, Marianne Williamson, Abraham Lincoln, Henry David Thoreau, John Shelby Spong, Deepak Chopra, Norman Vincent Peale, Robert Schuller, Iyanla Vanzant, Oprah Winfrey, Caroline Myss, Gerry Spence, Tina Turner, Ravi Shankar, Phillip C. McGraw, Rabbi Joseph Telushkin, Einstein,

George Soros, Maya Angelou, and Victor E. Frankl. Look at Helen Keller who had neither the "eyes" to see nor the "ears" to hear yet she *still* heard a different voice other than the voice of fear. Helen Keller knew no lack of love. All these people saw past the illusion of limitation. They saw past the illusion of fear. Instead they saw infinite love, infinite life, and infinite possibilities. All these people are examples of how it is possible to live in this world and still know God.

What is it in YOU that resists heeding the unspoken word of God? It can only be heard if you have the ears to hear. His "word" is in the stillness of the present. The present moment offers a silence that is supreme peace. In this state of peace we become aware of our divine nature that is aligned with Spirit. At last, we are One with God.

Why do we resist going from the body to the spirit? Our thought system will never admit there is a present. It would say, "Yes, there is a present" but that is only an idea of it. Our thoughts make projections into ideas or ideals. Then we become afraid. Fear is just another thought. It is projected onto something we "believe" is reality. We make up these belief systems and then we become afraid of them. We have lost sense of reality. If you just observe what is going on, then you are not just a body but an awareness. You are merely observing the world. Awareness is an Action without a reaction.

Unfortunately we are terribly confined by our conditioning. It is like you going back to your job. Nobody has to tell you to earn money, to buy food; so you go back to work. You go back to the yesterday, to its preferences, its choices, the good and the bad. Look at your thought system. Yet we remain unwilling to change. We need to discover our true function in the world otherwise we will never get to know the truth of "know thyself." We will never make contact with our Spirit. We will never know peace. Please don't just sit there and agree or disagree with me, go and find out. Do something NEW with your life, something that has VITALITY. For once, can you do something you have never done before? This could be something NEW! Do you have the determination to step into the gentle arms of the present? If you did you would be extending your Spirit to the edges of the furthest galaxies! You would be united with the stars.

There is no other function than to extend the Spirit, to extend Love. Everything else is provided. Can we step out of fear? Is there fear in the present? These are questions you should ask. The present has energy to keep us from deceiving ourselves. Our egos want activity to keep us thinking that we are "trying." Even Yoda said "Do or do not, there is no try."

We are distracted by self-improvement. You try to get to know God, but to really know Him, you have to still your mind. Otherwise God is just a belief, an idea, or a thought. He is not confined to our limited use of language or thought. God is beyond words. God is real and He is eternal.

In Truth there is only eternity, not time. We are part of eternity. But the time illusion keeps us very active and very busy. Activity gives us the feeling that we enjoy self-improvement, eating this, moving here, doing this job, standing on your head...or whatever. We want activity, not the space of silence and peace. Are you going to choose again? Will you choose the peace that silences the noise of our thoughts, our worries, our arrogance, our preoccupations and our fears?

Will you silence your thoughts? *You* cannot silence your thoughts because that is just another activity! It is an effort! Awareness requires no effort, only willingness. In other words, only through the awareness of God can your thoughts be brought to stillness. In that quietness, it is as if your mind goes "blank." Some call it being spaced out, meditation, or prayer. Whatever you call it, it uses silence as the communication medium between your mind and the mind of God. Within this space lies eternal Joy where fear is impossible.

Within this space lies the Holy Instant that is necessary for miracles to occur. Miracles occur involuntarily without any effort on your part. Miracles need only your willingness to see things a different way. A Holy Instant is one moment of peace that is impeccable. It is one sincere moment of prayer. It is quiet meditation. It is an awareness so sharp and vast that no thought or memory or projection can intrude upon it. It is very holy. We need to make contact with the Holy Spirit within the Holy Instant if we ever hope to get out of our prison of fearful thoughts.

Just being silent can bless mankind. It has its own effect and energy without you doing anything with your brain. Is that a relief or what?! You no longer have to *try to get to God. You no longer have to try to be holy because you already are.* You only have to let go of everything that is false. And the process of undoing illusions is no small undertaking, as we have seen!

There is nothing more superior than the silent mind. It wants nothing. It can only be forever grateful. When you are at peace nothing can disturb your gratefulness. There is something in you, the Spirit, that is not attached to anything manifested in this world. You are not here for the world, the world is here for you. Whatever comes to your attention, you respond to it. Now you have the space to give peace and the only thing you know is love.

If someone says something wicked, you know it is not true because you are created by God, by the Universe. You were not created from fear. You were created from Absolute Love. It has been a long journey on a truthless path, but now you can insist on not being deceived anymore.

We have to reverse our thinking processes. No one else is going to do it for you because *only you can do it.* You have the potential. Belief systems are vain attempts to "capture" God for ourselves by putting God in a very small box. Belief systems say: "I know and you don't." When you are in the present you don't even care who knows because you are not concerned with knowings and opinions.

All your seeking, your crystals, rituals, traditions, conventions, seminars, and conformity has covered up your own holiness because they are all someone else's opinion about who and what you are. Are you a rock? Are you a mantra? Are you a candle flame? Are you a book of prayers? *No!!!* You are the light of the world, a Spirit without opinion, an awareness without a belief system! No guru, no preacher, no religion can take that away from you.

You don't need to go and preach. God still loves you. Whether you change or not the present is still here. We invented time. In reality only eternity exists. It exists in the present moment. Yet we are constantly evading the present by thinking in terms of space, time, and the confines of language and belief systems. *What is more important than making contact with your own holiness?*

To stop this evading of the present we must have awareness. Awareness is not thought because it is silent. You are merely observing God's creation. Is there a better way to spend your "time?" You will be in awe. Do not allow your thoughts to distract you from the present. This is easier when you get plenty of rest. Thank God there's sleep! (And then there are the people who want to make money by interpreting your dreams. The thought and activity of money making never stops!)

Just *be aware.* That is the only responsibility we have. Allow the Holy Spirit to flow through you with its song of silence. It will cleanse you of all fears, wantings, knowings, and insecurities. You will no longer seek answers because you have only questions. When you are aware you no longer worry about how to make a living, because you *are living.* When you are aware you are One with God, your Creator. In this Holy space of Supreme Peace nothing can hurt you, for you are loved much more than any thought or any belief could ever let you know. In the present is the Supreme Truth untouched by words. In the present is all the love you could ever want. In the present is *everything.*

Remember that you are loved. *You are always loved.* Now you can rest assured in perfect peace; recognizing how boundless is all the love there is for you in all the universe. If you only knew What waits for you in the auspicious moment of the present. If you only knew Who takes care of everything for you in eternity. If you only knew that this is not the end of the journey but only the beginning.

In this "now" all things begin, which is in Love. In this "now" is the perfect moment, outside of time. In this "now" is the space for your everlasting peace and your absolute beauty. In this "now" you are an awareness as vast as the endless stream of galaxies that light up the sky! In this "now" the great heavens bow down to you, showering you with boundless Love. For in this "now" you will *know* that Love is by God. Right now, *you are in the now.* Right now *you have attention.*

And right *now… you are Love itself.*

May each day be special,
May good things happen to you,
May the smiles you share
Show others you care
Then your smile will come back to you.

Take good care on your journey.
Sometimes they're short, sometimes long.
Whenever the road becomes bumpy
Please remember my song:

Now go forth with your mission.
Remember to nourish your soul.
Everyday can be special
If you just make it so.

Linda Greep

~

So let's begin the journey home,
with awareness and peace for guides;
grace protecting us,
love enveloping us.
Let your soul turn into
an empty mirror
that reflects the present.
Now let silence speak,
and as that gift begins,
we'll start out.
If you see me, be careful.
Tell no one what you've seen.
Every question becomes an eye—
I don't mean of ordinary sight.
So, too, will your sight for
the wonder of the universe
see the invisible substance
that is love's greatest mystery.

God

e-Wisdom

...*The Kingdom of Heaven is Like a Net...*

Matthew @ 13:47 NIV

~

Guesswork and gut reaction have their place. Just not in your marketing plan. Veridiem. The truth. The whole truth. And more.

Veridiem.com

~

Rewarding relationships.

Netcentives.com

~

Sync is everything.

fusionOne.com

~

The revolution beckons.

get-socket.com

~

Where do you want to go today?

Microsoft

~

Double espresso or the new economy? What gets you wired?

Investec Asset Management

~

Your music. Your life.

Rio digital audio player

~

A new world. A new way.

marchFirst.com

~

I am not a piece of your inventory. I am not a pair of eyeballs to be captured or a consumer profile to be sold. I am an individual and you will respect my privacy. I will not be bartered, traded or sold.
On the Net I am in control.

zeroknowledge.com

~

It's one Net. Dive in.

Novell.com

~

No limits. On the edge.

Sho.com

~

Do less. Have more.

Realsimple.com

~

The global village is a digital community.
Modern technology presents us with enormous
opportunities that are not only material
but also spiritual.
The question now facing mankind is –
are we brave enough
to fully harness this potential?

Jeremy S. Gluck, Spiritech Virtual Foundation

~

What is digitalism?
The answer is, that Digitalism is an acceptance
of the state of your mind.

Digitalism (532,000 members worldwide)

~

There is no room in any heaven
(or corporation)
for wolves who sacrifice decent families,
both now and for many generations to come.

The Familycologists

~

Deus ex Machina

Motto for Technosophy

~

Your life, your choice.
It's really up to you.
We don't ask you to do anything special
but to relax and be yourself.
You don't need to pray or do special things
every day.
Your existence and search for your truth is
enough for us.
Enjoy what you have
and be happy
about the little things
that can happen to you.
The more details you uncover in life,
the nearer you are to the truth.
We discovered that life is
so much easier to live
if you bring joy, happiness and
compassion to your surroundings.
It's up to you…

Digitalism

~

Are you going to wait? Still?
Because I refuse.
I refuse to watch this happen anymore.
I refuse to be a victim.
I don't know how I am supposed
to change the world,
But I will.
I am not going to stand by any longer
and watch my generation
flush society down the toilet.
The streets aren't safe,
Parks aren't safe,
homes aren't safe,
and now schools aren't safe.
There is something wrong with this picture.
And I feel sorry for those
that don't see it.
But most of all I pity those that do but choose to ignore it.
I am making a vow to myself to
stand up against it,
to make a difference,
and pray I am not alone.
My name is Jason Martin
from Littleton, Colorado.
I would like to send prayers out to my friends who were in
Columbine H.S.
I would like everyone to please say a prayer for the safety of
everyone who was
involved in this terrible tragedy…
let us all come together and pray
that this tragedy ends soon.

"A Message from Our Youth" by Jason Martin
e-mail received Monday, 24 April 2000

~

More than 70,000 people in 83 countries
Around the world
Committed to the same ideals.
We think and act as one.

ArthurAnderson.com

~

Contradictions in the Bible

I am asked many times in my debates with
Christains to demonstrate some
contradictions in the Bible. Here I have laid out 70
of them. I have broken them up
into 5 categories:

Contradictions on God
Contradictions on Law
Contradictions on Names or Numbers
Contradictions Based on Different Authors
Contradictions That Are Just Silly

Cygnus
www.cygnus-study.com/pagecon.shtml

~

The 10 Core Rules of Netiquette:

Remember the Human.

Adhere to the same standards of behavior online that you follow in real life.

Know where you are in cyberspace.

Respect other people's time and bandwidth.

Make yourself look good online.

Share expert knowledge.

Help keep flame wars under control.

Respect other people's privacy.

Don't abuse your power.

Be forgiving of other people's mistakes.

www.albion.com/netiquette/corerules.html

A Message from the UnderGround!

The UnderGround always wins: from Moses to Tom Green, it's
the outsiders, the rebels, the iconoclasts and the waterballoon
throwers who keep things interesting.
Because unlike the mass-produced,
mass-marketed crapola that bends over backwards to please
everyone,
the UnderGround doesn't give a damn.
It isn't afraid to be provocative, challenging,
and unpredictable...
They make the rules,
and then they break them.
And now the UGO.com 16th Annual
UnderGround Open seeks to salute the maniacs, visionaries,
and screwballs who inspire the great, frighten the weak, and
make up for the corporate-media broadblah
that's been gumming up the works.
Hey, it's the least we could do.
We're UGO.com, and we're just trying to make sure The Man
doesn't do to the UnderGround
what The Man did to Times Square.

We Are The New Civilization

We are here.
We are waking up now, out of the past,
To a bigger dream.
We are friends and equals,
We are diverse and unique,
And we're united for something
Bigger than differences.
We believe in freedom and cooperation,
Abundance and harmony.
We are a culture emerging,
A renaissance of the
Essence of humanity.
We find our guidance,
And we discern our own truth.
We go in many directions,
Yet we refuse to disperse.
We have many names,
We speak many languages.
We are local, we are global.
We are in all regions of the world,
We're everywhere in the air.
We are the universe being aware of itself,
We are the wave of evolution.
We are in every child's eyes,
We face the unknown with
Wonder and excitement.
We are messengers from the future,
Living in the present.
We come from silence,
And we speak our truth.
We cannot be quieted,
Because our voice is within everyone...

We have no enemies,
No boundaries can hold us.
We respect the cycles and expressions
Of nature, because we are nature.
We don't play to win,
We play to live and learn.
We act out of inspiration,
Love, and integrity.
We explore, we discover, we feel,
And we laugh.
We are building a world
That works for
EVERYONE.
We endeavor to live our lives to the
FULLEST POTENTIAL.
We are Independent,
Self-sufficient,
And Responsible.
We relate to each other in
PEACE,
With compassion and respect,
We Unite in Community.
We celebrate the wholeness
Within and around us All.
We dance to the rhythm of creation.
We weave the threads of new times.
We are
The New Civilization.

www.newciv.org/ncn/weare.html

Notes

Notes

Notes

Notes

Notes

Notes

Notes

Ordering Additional Copies

To order additional copies of this book:

- Call toll-free (800) 932-5420

- Order from Greenleaf Book Group website at:
  www.greenleafenterprises.com

- Complete the form below and mail it to:

  Preferred Customer Dept.
  Greenleaf Book Group LLC
  660 Elmwood Point
  Aurora, OH   44202

$14.95 ($12.95 + $2 S&H) x _____ = _____

Name _____

Address _____

City _____

State _____ Zip Code _____

Phone _____ Fax _____

Email _____

Pay by: ❑Check   ❑Visa   ❑MC   ❑AmEx   ❑Disc

CC # _____

Exp Date _____ Signature _____

Ordering Additional Copies

To order additional copies of this book:

- Call toll-free (800) 932-5420

- Order from Greenleaf Book Group website at:
  www.greenleafenterprises.com

- Complete the form below and mail it to:

   Preferred Customer Dept.
   Greenleaf Book Group LLC
   660 Elmwood Point
   Aurora, OH   44202

$14.95 ($12.95 + $2 S&H) x _____ = _____

Name _____

Address _____

City _____

State _____ Zip Code _____

Phone _____ Fax _____

Email _____

Pay by: ❏Check   ❏Visa   ❏MC   ❏AmEx   ❏Disc

CC # _____

Exp Date _____ Signature _____